The Amazing Middle East

Travels Through Israel, Jordan and Egypt

March-April 2012

By

Laurie Holden

Phoenix, 2014

The Amazing Middle East

Travels Through Israel, Jordan and Egypt

Copyright © 2014, 2017. All rights reserved.

Published by CreateSpace Independent Publishing Platform

Second Paperback Edition, October 2017

ISBN: 978-1978356313
ISBN: 1978356315

I wish to thank Louis Morgan and my daughter Ilana Lydia, herself an author, for their important support and suggestions.

Wednesday, March 14, 2012 & Thursday the 15th

Up at 3am   Ilana cooked breakfast. The Supershuttle was early; the driver, after asking where I was traveling to, said he had been to Petra and talked about riding down on either a horse or camel. The lady behind me was going to Vegas, her daughter showing horses there at the Arena.

At the terminal at Phoenix' Sky Harbor I soon found Louis.

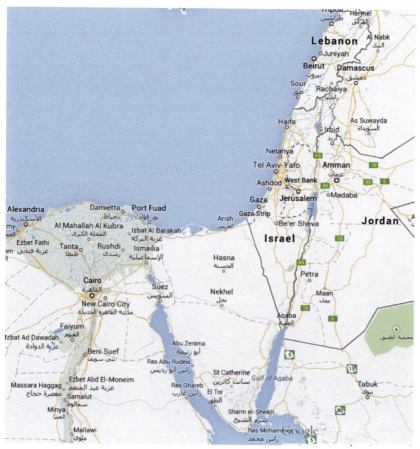

There was a problem with the tickets but it was soon resolved.

We sat next to Guy on the plane, an interesting fellow who spends almost all his spare time listening to lectures on tape on many, many topics. He was a mechanical engineer with a minor in languages, and he was also a marathon runner. He didn't socialize much but had been married thirty-three years. When we mentioned Petra he remarked how he wanted to do the marathon there! Louis asked him for his email address but he didn't want to give it to him, explaining, rather lamely, that since he only knew him this short time that he'd just have to sit at his computer trying to make up things to say. It was clear that there wasn't much spare room in his private world.

We arrived at JFK around 11:30am; I was dizzy getting off the plane but my cane helped. Fortunately, the dizziness soon went away on terra firma. We were facing a seven hour wait so went into a Chili's there in the terminal. I had an ice tea and chicken enchilada soup and Louis went for chili and a salad. After that there was reading time so I pulled one of the two books I'd bought along, Clive Cussler's *Valhalla Rising*. (The other book, *The Greatest Music Stories Never Told* by Rick Beyer I worked on intermittently with the Cussler.)

Later on I had a Starbucks ice coffee. We were both relieved to board our second flight. On the long flight to Tel Aviv our seatmate was a young man named Samuel who had dual Israeli and U.S. citizenship, and had served in the Israel army. A Jewish family sat a few seats away with a quiet baby. My perennially itchy lower right leg was acting up again.

ISRAEL

How good it is to arrive after a long flight! We landed at the Ben Gurion Airport, not only the air transportation hub for Tel Aviv, but for Israel as a whole. We were picked up by Rafi and we loaded our luggage in his Nissan; he spoke three languages, saying that many people in Israel did so. Twenty percent of the population is Muslim, he said.

We got to our Mecure Hotel at 7:15am (Thursday) Phoenix time. Israeli time was ten hours earlier. It was a nice clean hotel with a split-level lobby and free internet: I was able to shoot off a quick note to Ilana and Amy of our safe arrival.

Louis was able to get a voucher for supper after he had the hotel call the tour company to verify that we had paid for the service.

As it was late afternoon we decided to walk down to see the Mediterranean Sea before it got dark and have supper afterwards. It wasn't far and there were breakers washing against the beach. Louis walked up the beach a ways getting pictures; I took mine basically in one spot. There was a couple of interesting high-rises plus a large hole which was the foundation of a new one under construction that we had passed. Later I read on Wikipedia that Tel Aviv has "the world's largest concentration of Bauhaus buildings." Itzhak Perlman was born here. Tel Aviv is nicknamed "The White City," "The City That Never Sleeps," and "Sin City".

We watched the sunset over the sea. Wow – it was gorgeous! Here we were on the east end of the Mediterranean Sea - in the Levant, the Orient – an area of the world bursting with history and a place called many names over the millennia. Walking back to our hotel Louis noticed the American flag up one of the side streets and said he bet that would be the U.S. embassy. So we followed the hill up and it was. Louis started taking pictures and a guard approached and told him: "No pictures!" Louis isn't one to discourage easily so as I started back towards the hotel he moved only a little ways and made sure the guard was out of sight before resuming his picture taking. I walked back and told him that with all the unrest in this country that he shouldn't be messing around – that the next warning might be a bullet zinging past his head. As I said, he doesn't discourage easily so proceeded to take many more pictures than he first intended and caught up to me a few minutes later.

We ate at the Viking Restaurant which served Russian cuisine. Louis loved his borscht; I had lentil soup and chicken stroganoff – both very good.

Friday 16th

We were up in time to enjoy a wonderful breakfast. At the allotted time our tour van arrived. Alex was our tour guide. There were four others in our tour group: Silvana and Andre who were newlyweds from Brazil, Willodean from Indiana and Julie from Houston.

Alex said Israel was about the size of New Jersey and had seven million people, 1.5 of them in Tel Aviv. It was the second largest city in Israel – Jerusalem being the largest. As we all headed to Jaffa, he said that Jaffa excavations show it has been occupied from 7,500 years before the common era; a wall was built around the city 500 years ago. Jonah sailed from here to meet his whale. Jaffa is also famous for other biblical stories from Solomon and Peter. The Ottomans ruled this area from 1515 until the British captured it in WW1. In 1948 Israel gained its independence from Britain.

Alex led us around the top of Jaffa Hill via its ancient, narrow streets, descending stone steps, ascending others. Today most of the residents here in the old town are artists and professionals and we saw a number of signs over doors. We also had great views to the harbor and Tel Aviv not far away up the coast. And we could see the Andromeda Rocks just a few meters from shore:

The mythical story goes that her mother Cassiopeia boasted that her daughter was more beautiful than the Nereids, the nymph-daughters of the sea god Nereus. To punish the queen for her arrogance, Poseidon, brother to Zeus and god of the sea, sent a sea monster named Cetus to ravage the coast including the kingdom of the vain queen. The desperate king consulted the

Oracle who announced that no respite would be found until he sacrificed his daughter, Andromeda, to the monster. Stripped naked, she was chained to a rock on the coast. Perseus happened upon the chained Andromeda and killed the sea monster. He set Andromeda free, and married her.[1]

When we returned close to where we were parked we went by the Clock Tower and were delighted with the zodiac statues beside the beautiful nineteenth century Franciscan Church of St. Peter at Kedumim Square. Both pictures below by Louis.

Back in Alex's van, we descended Jaffa Hill, passed by Tel Aviv and headed north. "Three hundred years ago the population of Israel was only three hundred thousand people," Alex said. "This area was very arid and water was in short supply."

'I am the rose of Sharon, and the lily of the valleys' sang Solomon in the Song of Songs. Sharon is the most fertile part of Israel's coastal plain, extending about fifty miles from Tel Aviv-Jaffa to the foothills of Mount Carmel."[2] Environments change and over the centuries since biblical times the area turned into a treeless prairie with barren soil and marshes, said Alex, and that pioneers a hundred and fifty years ago started to re-farm the land but found they had to plant special trees to suck up the swamps. According to an internet article, *Eucalyptus camaldulensis* trees were brought in from Australia in the late 19th century, and were

---

[1] http://en.wikipedia.org/wiki/Andromeda_(mythology)
[2] Caesarea, Pictorial Guide, (Herzila, Israel, Palphot, n.d.), p 24-5

used especially because of their reputation as "dryer of swamps". They were easy to reproduce and grow and were second only to *Pinus halepensis* as "the most commonly planted tree in Israel"[3] Finally, Alex explained, after outbreaks of malaria the Jewish settlers decided to drain the swamps in the 1920's and 30's.

A ways north of Tel-Aviv Alex pointed to the left saying that in Herzliya Pituach there were many resorts. The area was named for the 'Father of Zionism,' Theodor Herzl.

He talked a minute or two about what has been going on in Israel, his thoughts divided between driving and what he was saying, concluding rather obliquely that politics here are not that innocent.

We passed by Netanya, a city famous for its diamond processing. We were travelling the *Via Maris*, an ancient trade route by the sea that began in the late Bronze Age and runs from Egypt to kingdoms north of Israel. Over the centuries there have been several improvements of course.

King Herod's time had creative art. Alex referred to Herod as "a crazy king but a major builder" and he decided in 22 BCE to build a modern model city to rival Rome and name it after his benefactor and boss, August Caesar – thus Caesarea. He selected a settlement called Straton's Tower originally made a few centuries earlier by the Phoenicians, neighbors just to the north from what is now Lebanon. The area had a deep harbor and he wanted to make his new city an international seaport – which indeed it became.

Subsequently, Herod employed the best engineers and architects of the day and created an enclosed harbor 275 by 500 meters long[4] which was a unique masterpiece of the day. (This involved creating the two permanent breakwaters using wood frames floated into position and filling them with a concrete made of

---

[3] http://www.wildflowers.co.il/kkl/english/plant.asp?ID=1072
[4] Measurements varied in the sources I read.

lime and a type of volcanic ash mixed with rock and rubble – they were rocking 'n' rolling – and sinking them down to the seabed.)

Although Caesarea served as a major seaport in its day, a fault line runs just along the coast and over the years earthquakes have devastated most of the seawalls, as it did the magnificent palace Herod built as his administrative capital over the land (but is now reclaimed by the sea). Greeks and Romans had come in numbers to the city, it reaching a population of twelve thousand during this period making it quite cosmopolitan. At its peak, it became the largest city in Judea with 125,000.[5]

Over the decades Caesarea's majority population became Greek causing the Jewish minority to tire of foreign leaders and occupation and in 66 CE (common era) a rebellion against Rome ensued, triggering Emperor Vespasian to send his son Titus (who was known to have a personality disorder) to deal with the rebels which culminated with the destruction of the Second Temple in Jerusalem and the Masada massacre in 73. (More about Masada later.)

We entered Caesarea through the south gate and the first thing we saw was the 3000-seat theater on the sea. It was a clear and blustery day and the view of this relatively well-preserved huge theater against the blue sky and sea was quite impressive. The semi-circular seats are intact and indeed the venue is popular for contemporary concerts (even if they play Bach!) Alex told us the niches were for the prompters.

When we left the theater we walked through an area of broken columns and statutes. Alex said of the de-headed statues that the Muslims chopped off all the heads as they were uncovered. A little later he revised that statement by allowing that some large statues were made headless so that new heads could be put on as political climates changed. For some reason my camera didn't work here – but Louis' did:

---

[5] http://en.wikipedia.org/wiki/Caesarea_Maritima

The huge amphitheater   All that's left of Herod's palace

We walked along the hippodrome where horses were raced and later gladiator games were performed for audiences of fifteen thousand. In the distance we could see the remains of the Crusader castle from the period 1099 to 1291.[6]

After we got back to Alex's van and he counted six sightseers we travelled a mile or two up the road to see one of the aqueducts and the section we saw looked in good condition. Alex said the aqueduct was built in two stages and that there had been ten Roman legions posted here by the sea presumably to oversee the construction as well as maintain security for the area.

Our van pushed on to the Jezreel Valley and the ancient ruins at Megiddo.

Caesarea had its up and downs over the centuries but at the end of the thirteenth century the Muslim Mamluks invaded and completely destroyed it. After that smaller, incidental groups occupied the area until the modern excavation began.

As we drove by a kibbutz Alex told us gas costs twice what it does in the U.S.; Julie who had recently been in Norway, said gas was $15 a gallon there!

---

[6] "When King Baldwin I took Caesarea in 1101, he massacred both the Arab and Jewish inhabitants…Caesarea, Ibid, p 17.

Alex said Arabs don't believe in apartments, preferring to live in family units.

Our tour was supposed to include Haifa and the Baha'i Shrine but didn't, and Louis argued with Alex whose instructions were different than what we had been promised. Louis was correct but he had a problem letting the issue go and the loud discussion continued the next day. It was starting to upset the other passengers: one even told me she was getting knots in her stomach. In his defense, seeing Haifa had been one of his main goals for the trip. Our tour company had subcontracted the whole tour, and we found a lot of the drawbacks of not having someone who worked for the tour company being with us and overseeing the trip.

We traveled by Mt. Carmel on our way to the Valley of Armageddon. Armageddon is the Greek work for Megiddo, the ancient dig site we would spend the afternoon at. So far, the earliest traces of humanity in this ancient city date back to the sixth millennium BCE; excavation has revealed twenty-five cities – or separate civilizations - at this sight. That's humbling to think about. You and your ancestors having a nice little city, important in its time, and then something happens: a fatal war, plague, a destroying earthquake – no one or almost no one is left. Decades or centuries pass and new folks see advantage of settling on this hill beside Armageddon Valley. Twenty-five times.

The first written source of Megiddo "and the first recorded battle in history" – dates…to a detailed account of the 1479 BCE campaign of Pharaoh Thutmose III to reassert Egypt's dominion over territories in Canaan.[7] (Details of the battle are carved into the walls at Karnak which we would visit later.) The city is

---

[7] Vamosh, Miriam Feinberg, *Megiddo, Armageddon*, Israel Antiquities Authority, ERETZ, 1997, p 3.

mentioned in the Bible eleven times[8] and was key in Solomon's day. In 732 BCE it was destroyed by the Assyrians who built a new city. During the Roman era it was a garrison post; Napoleon defeated the Turks near Megiddo, and in 1918 the third (and final) Battle of Megiddo, the Allies defeated the Ottomans. And in 1948 the Arabs were also defeated here, and in 1949 Kibbutz- Megiddo was established just west of the tell. *The Book of Revelation* has the final battle between good and evil, right here, at Armageddon…

King David's city was at the 16th level, but four centuries before Christ it was abandoned.

We parked and went into the visitor's center. I saw a couple of books on local history I wanted and asked Alex if we would be returning through here. He said we wouldn't so I bought them. Our group proceeded to climb the winding path to the top of the tell. Past the Bronze Age gates, Solomon's Gate, the Massebot Shrine, the granary and stables. We saw a little of the excavated grid system – one of the earliest examples of a grid system – established so long ago by the Assyrians. Some of the places had life-sized wire statues of animals showing where they were fed and housed.

During Megiddo's many sieges, ultimately their most vulnerable point was their water supply. It was outside their gates so the enemy could cut them off from it. In the ninth century BCE they figured out what to do to secure their water: at the southwest segment inside the walls they bored a hole thirty-five meters deep to an underground spring.

Left below, a model of the city from 1457 BCE.[9] Right, stairs descending to the well:

---

[8] Ibid, p 10.

[9] http://en.wikipedia.org/wiki/File:Model_of_Megiddo,_1457_BCE..jpg

Alex showed us where the entrance to the well shaft was and told us to follow it down and continue the path outside where he would meet us with his van.

We soon reached the steps leading steeply down to the well that at one time had been secret. There were modern steel steps in place today or I'm doubtful if I could have made it; as it was, the descent was daunting and dangerous and slippery and low lighting yielded creepy shadows and poor visibility. Already shaky from climbing up and around the tell in touring, I held onto the damp metal banister as I checked each step down to verify its grip, the steps seemed to go on and on as the bottom eluded sight and it became increasingly colder and one could hear trickles of water from the sides. It was hundred and fifteen feet down before we reached the well itself which was maybe twenty feet across inside a dark, dripping cave. Then there were steps up. Some of them were steep, but there was daylight at the top and I would have traded all my gold for a good horizontal path! Julie had graciously taken the books I had purchased to help. And that was a *great* help. Thank you again, Julie!

I was totally exhausted when I climbed into Alex's van.

Mary Magdalene some think she was born in Megiddo. Alex mentioned James Michener's *The Source* and how it said that most conquered lands 'adopted the Gods of the winner' – but the Jews didn't, and they suffered.

What happened to the Jews that they needed a state created for them in the twentieth century? A lot. Their history has filled hundreds of volumes as it should but as this is a surfing journal, only the highest of the highlights will be skimmed. Starting with the 6th century BCE conquest of their land by Babylon and the destruction of the First Temple, Jews were expelled from the population, as recorded in the Bible. From 597 BCE onwards, there were three distinct groups of Hebrews: a group in Babylon and, a group in Judaea, and another group in Egypt. This disbursement became known as the diaspora.[10]

In 635 CE, the region was conquered by Arabs and it remained under Muslim control for the next 1300 years. In 1095 Pope Urban II proclaimed the first crusade, with the stated goal of restoring Christian access to the holy places.[11] There were economic opportunities too, but one is not supposed to think about that. Over the next few centuries there were lots of crusades, battles, slaying and heroes made like Richard the Lionhearted. It was such cheerio business back then.

The last battle of the crusades was fought in Acre, a port city just north of Haifa in 1291, Alex said. Acre is one of the oldest continuously inhabited sites in the world, which we would likely have seen if he had taken us to Haifa.

In 1799 Napoleon set his sights on Acre and "voiced his conviction that a mere two weeks would be necessary to capture the linchpin of his conquest of the Holy Land before marching on to Jerusalem. ... However, the troops under the capable Jezzar Pasha, refusing to surrender, withstood the siege for one and a half months"[12] before Napoleon decided *This was not working*, and left to bother folks somewhere else.

Since the Diaspora, some Jews have aspired to return to "Zion" and the "Land of Israel". The first wave of modern Jewish migration to Ottoman-ruled Palestine, known as the First Aliyah, began in 1881, as Jews fled pogroms in Eastern Europe. Although Theodor Herzl is credited with founding political

---

[10] http://en.wikipedia.org/wiki/Jewish_diaspora
[11] The Muslim rulers at the time were denying Christians access to the holy sites.
[12] http://en.wikipedia.org/wiki/Siege_of_Acre_(1799)

Zionism, a movement which sought to establish a Jewish state in the Land of Israel had been around for some time.

At the beginning of the twentieth century it was the Ottomans in charge. In 1917, at the end of World War I, England conquered Palestine, and in that year as well Prime Minister Lord Balfour promised the Jews "a national home in Palestine." And in 1922 the League of Nations granted Britain a mandate over Palestine. Additional aliyahs and the aftermath of the First World War brought hundreds of thousands more to Israel sparking the Arab Revolt of 1936-39. The threat of a Jewish State in their midst caused the countries of the Middle-East to form an Arab League as early as 1945 to establish a united front.

In 1947 the United Nations recommended the making of an Israeli state. This precipitated the Arab-Israeli War of 1948 (also known as the War of Independence) in which Jordan took the West Bank and Egypt the Gaza Strip. The end of this war, May 15, 1948, marked the beginning of the Israeli State. And finally a year later Israel was admitted to the UN as an independent, but reduced, state.[13]

Right away the new nation built up its military and in 1956 they tested their might by occupying the Gaza Strip for a brief time. In June 1967 they initiated the Six Day War in which they regained control of the Gaza Strip and the West Bank, took the Golan Heights – and for good measure grabbed the Sinai Peninsula, a chunk of land more than double the size of Israel itself (but later gave it back in a peace agreement.)

The Six Day War did not settle matters between Israel, Palestine and their neighbors. Skirmishes and terrorists attacks still continue. For every bit of righteousness there's an equal measure of blame on both sides.

---

[13] http://en.wikipedia.org/wiki/Israel#Zionism_and_the_British_mandate

As we pushed on to the city of Tiberius where we would spend the night, Alex told us that the Sea of Galilee was also known as Kinneret and Lake Tiberius and is 696 feet below sea level. And the Golan Heights lay on the northeast side.

Our Leonardo Hotel room had a very nice view of the Sea. (Strangely, sitting in the room's chair, the sea view was obliterated by the window's design with a broad, horizontal metal strip covering the city and sea front! One had to stand and look through the upper part to appreciate the wonderful view.) At supper we couldn't get milk or coffee because it was the Sabbath.

Speaking of the Sabbath, we found the Sabbath elevator very intriguing. Apparently, pushing buttons is not allowed on this day, so one elevator was fixed to automatically go from floor to floor, stopping at each so no buttons need be pushed!

Louis wanted to find a place to buy Cokes and rum and went out exploring after supper. Ordinarily I would have gone with him but I was exhausted from the day's activities.

Saturday 17th

Breakfast was rather institutional. Until the 1967 war the Golan Heights was owned by Syria. Alex said they had plans to divert the Jordan River which would have caused the Sea of Galilee to dry up – and this was one of the prime instigations of the war. Also, Egyptian President Abdel Nasser apparently said he was "willing to lose a million Egyptians to destroy Israel." The Six Day War ended in the Golan Heights.

Alex talked a little about Christian Jews who are ethnic Jews who have converted to Christianity: of course in the earliest years they were the only Christians. He went on to tell us about Josephus who was a first century Roman-Jewish general who had led the Jewish forces against Vespasian near Galilee. He was captured by the Roman general but later let go. Eventually, he became the most important scholar and historian of the time. It was from him we learned the amazing story of the Masada siege – of which there will be more later.[14]

We drove to the Mountain of Beatitudes. This was my favorite spot in Israel. It was a warm, bright day and such a beautiful area with the tasteful octagonal Church of the Beatitudes with its green dome surrounded by trees, hedges and benches overlooking the bright blue of the Sea of Galilee – an island in green pastures. Most of the important churches with all their grand art we saw in Israel didn't have an iota of the peace and warmth of this Beatitudes setting. The words of Christ's sermon seemed embedded in the very earth as they were engraved in the stones along the walkways. You can feel them without listening. The church marks the spot where Christ delivered his sermon.

I walked through the surrounding colonnaded cloisters into the church itself. How clean and simple it was – very different from the busy ornateness of the other cathedrals we had visited. It was a place of reflection. Outside, I sat on a bench for a few minutes just taking it all in. Part of the time there was a chorus practicing under some trees a little further up the hill. Before we departed we heard bells toll.

---

[14] A mathematical game of chance is named after Josephus based upon an actual happening: "According to Josephus' account of the siege of Yodfat, he and his 40 soldiers were trapped in a cave, the exit of which was blocked by Romans. They chose suicide over capture and decided that they would form a circle and start killing themselves using a step of three. Josephus states that by luck or possibly by the hand of God, he and another man remained the last, and gave up to the Romans." http://en.wikipedia.org/wiki/Josephus_problem

We proceeded a very short distance to Tabgha (almost at the base of the Beatitudes). This is not a village but a green valley next to the Sea of Galilee. The Benedictines have built the Church of the Multiplication of the Loaves and Fishes which we walked through. They maintain a large monastery next door. And next to the shore of the sea is the small, black Church of the Primacy of St. Peter, built in 1933 on traces of a fourth-century church on the spot where it is believed Jesus appeared to his disciples after his resurrection.

We vanned two miles over to Capernaum where Christ lived after Nazareth. For the last hundred years the Franciscans have been excavating the ancient town. About twelve thousand people had lived there, so it was large. Today there is an open-air museum, gardens, statutes and a modern round church over part of the excavations, and inside, this memorial had clean simplicity too, and windows all around to see the excavations outside; in the center of this quiet place an open area allows you to look down upon the ruins of what is believed to be St. Peter's house.

On the way into the Memorial we had passed through the gardens with a beautiful statue of St. Peter, and, nearby, a low stone fence, each stone carved deeply with designs, one of them depicting the Ark of the Covenant. Then we examined the ruins of the old synagogue, some of its marble walls and columns still standing. Beyond the walls we could see the modern red domes of a Greek Orthodox church.

Pictured below: *left*, statue of St. Peter; *center*, Arch of the Covenant; *right*, remains of the house of St. Peter

Next, Alex drove us into the Golan Heights, passing by land mine fields. There were warning signs along the road about them. The countryside was bare, rolling hills. After a while we seemed to definitely be climbing a mountain. Later I was able to determine it was Mt. Bental (3482 feet high). In 1973 Syria and Egypt attacked: this is known as the Yon Kippur War, and lasted seventeen days. The area between Mt. Bental and Mt. Hermon was the scene of a massive invasion from Syria of 1500 tanks and a thousand other pieces of heavy artillery. Israel fought with only 160 tanks.[15] After fierce fighting the Syrians finally retreated. The area between the two mountains is now known as the Valley of Tears.

We parked near the summit and only had to walk the last three or four hundred feet. It was rather bracingly chilly on this mountain top. What used to be an Israeli army camp with trenches and artillery mounts is now a public park. Cut-out statutes of action soldiers helped illustrate the area's historical significance. A modern restaurant and store called *Kofi Anan* meaning *'Coffee of the Clouds'* provided us with good food while

---

[15]

http://www.jewishvirtuallibrary.org/jsource/Society_&_Culture/geo/bental.html

enjoying a great view. We sat as a group including Silvana and Andre but without Louis who decided to go without lunch to take many pictures.

Along the road from the parking area to the summit are wonderful metal sculptures – art that helps create a healthy, lighter perspective to this area with its serious past.

On the way down the Golan Heights as we approached the Jordan River, Andre asked Alex if he would stop for a few minutes in the park; and Andre agreed to pay the entrance fee. Subsequently he drove us into a park and we walked a short distance to the river. It was smaller than I anticipated, being more a *stream* by the standards we used when I was growing up in Maine. Alex said it was larger at the southern outlet of the Sea of Galilee, and that was the location used in the biblical baptisms. Nevertheless, the water was flowing strongly, and I think we all stuck our hand in to feel its historical charge.

There were peacocks in the park and I got a picture of one, but when back in the van and turning around someone spotted a male spreading his feathers in a fan to attract a nearby female. We all watched as they got together, a show not worth writing home about, which I didn't, only relegating it these notes of documentation.

On our way back down to Tiberius following along on the west side of the Sea of Galilee Alex gave us some other bits of history, much of which I lost due to the swaying van and trying to figure out the words I missed. However, I did get that "Bethany" means love of the poor. And the use of incense goes back to times of sacrifice, to help cover the smells.

We visited the Galilee Boat Museum which houses among other exhibits, an ancient boat which could have been used by Jesus during his fishing days. There were some interesting sculptures outside the museum as well.

After that Alex returned us to our respective hotels in Tiberius. Julie and Willodean had chosen "A" class hotels but the rest of us had opted for "B." Nevertheless, all our hotels were good-to-excellent.

Sunday 18th

We packed our suitcases in Alex's van as we would not be returning to Tiberius. We stopped at Cana and visited the Franciscan Church of the Miracle built at the spot where Christ turned water into wine at a wedding feast. This was his first miracle and it has always seemed odd to me that he should have chosen this to be his first. But maybe he wanted to test his power on something that didn't really matter, in case it didn't work quite right.

On the walk back to the van Louis spotted a street kiosk selling Pomegranate drinks and several people partook. There were also one dollar shopping bags with beautiful designs: I bought one or two for gifts as did others.

Our van took us to Nazareth, a bustling city of eighty thousand and known as the Arab capital of Israel. Nazareth is thought to be the home of Mary, and where she was told by an angel that she would bear a blessed son; and it is the traditional boyhood home of Christ. The current church - Basilica of Annunciation - was constructed in 1969 over the site of earlier Byzantine-era and then Crusader-era churches,[16] plus two others. Inside, the lower level contains the Grotto of the Annunciation, believed by many Christians to be the remains of the original childhood home of Mary. Alex said it was the largest basilica in Asia Minor.

The door to the Basilica was a beautiful carved and polished depicting scenes from the life of Christ. Along the street in front was a billboard saying, "And whoever seeks a religion other than Islam, it will never be accebted [sic] of Him, and in the Hereafter he will be one of the losers."

I took several pictures of the wonderful bas-relief door, but my pictures inside, especially of the grotto didn't come out too well.

Nearby was St. Joseph's Church and we also went inside it. It stands on the area thought to be Joseph's workshop.

As we were walking back to our vehicle Alex indicated we could go into the bakery we were in front of if we'd like a break. At the Mlahroum Bakery I treated Julie to coffee and cake. Willodean, and then Alex joined us at our table. Louis was getting pictures of all the amazing displays of goodies. I learned that Julie was an accountant for a Houston firm that often handled foreign oil accounts which required her to travel. She was divorced and her children were living on their own at this point. Being with her I couldn't help but wish that we both lived in the same city. (After the trip she emailed me that she had spent a couple of weeks in Angola, a location that didn't invite touring.)

Willodean's job was unusual: she worked for a truck and large recreational vehicles distributorship, delivering the rigs to all corners of the country. The couple from Brazil, both polite and quiet folks, were very much in love with each other and lived in their private world. He had lived in Israel previously and on

---

[16] http://en.wikipedia.org/wiki/Basilica_of_the_Annunciation

several occasions on the tour asked Alex to take us a mile or two off his planned route to briefly visit something he knew about.

The coffee break with Julie and Willodean was fun. I learned that Turkish pastry is called Knauffe.

Alex mentioned that we weren't far from the ancient city of Samaria and Mt. Gilboa: the latter was where King Saul – Israel's first monarch - was defeated by the Philistines and fell on his sword.

About fifteen miles to the southeast of Megiddo is the Beit She'an National Park. Before we entered the park we had lunch outside at a falafel stand in the town of Beit She'an – an interesting experience.

These ruins are the largest excavation site in Israel. An open trailer-train took us from the information center into the excavation area and out. The dig was probably a half-mile across and there were numerous paths to follow and ruins to study including some catacombs, temples, a bathhouse, a theater and more. There was a lot to see here and National Park personnel had taken pains to make touring the ruins interesting to families. There were cartoon character figures here and there. There were also life-sized black cut-out figures of dancing women or women just sightseeing. Here's some pictures Louis took:

People have lived in Beit She'an for 7000 years and the excavation of the tell show eighteen different towns. The city was built on a rise between two streams. During the reign of

King Solomon it was under Israelite control and remained so until the Assyrians conquered the area in 732 BCE; soon it virtually ceased to exist. It was not resettled until Alexander the Great conquered the area and for the next 900 years was known as Scythopolis and prospered under Roman rule.[17]

An earthquake in 749 greatly damaged the city. The Arabs rebuilt it (calling it Beisan) and then the Crusaders had it but were soon evicted by the Mamluks in 1263 and it reverted to Muslim rule. Muhammad Ali, the ruler of Egypt took over the area in 1830 but during the Israeli War of Independence in 1949 most of the Arabs fled and an Israeli government was set up.[18]

I didn't do a third of the exploration that Louis and the rest of the group did. I had banged the shin of my left leg a second time getting in or out of Alex's Chevy van. (I do take issue with the designers of that van, who made a double step move out from underneath whenever the van side door opened. This was good: the problem was that the top step was silver – easy to see – and the bottom one was flat black, not easy to see, especially with my bifocals.) The second bump had broken the skin and it was hurting and very raw. I wanted to return in hopes of finding some Band-Aids in the store at the entrance.

On the way out of the area I grabbed a seat among a group – I would soon learn - were LDSers. A scene played out around me as sometimes does in life. An older man sitting immediately to my right said with smiling paternalism to a teenage girl opposite me: "You come visit us and we'll have you married in two months!" to which she gave a sort of wiggling jump, exclaiming "Tee Hee Hee!" Like clockwork, her mother sitting next to her gave an identical wiggling jump also exclaiming 'Tee Hee!'

I did get the Band-Aids and when the others had finished exploring we vanned to another dig that was about five miles

---

[17] Beit She'an, Capital of the Decapolis, p. 2
[18] Ibid, p 5

away, Beit Alfa, as a request from Andre. He had once been a member of this kibbutz. The synagogue there was built in the sixth century but discovered in 1928. It is remarkable for its mosaic floor which has three main panels, the first, the Ark of the Covenant between two menorah, the second is a zodiac wheel and the last the sacrifice of Isaac. Louis reminded me that Roman and Greek elements had been incorporated into the zodiac in Jewish context.

From here we journeyed to the beleaguered city of Jerusalem where we would spend the next three nights and where we got a good exposure of the Islamic call to prayers issuing five times a day from the nearest minaret. At first it was startling, but I soon came to enjoy the humbling interruptions to our busy touring for their presence, their sad soulful subservience to God, their emanation of peace, calling forth, by the muezzin the adhan, their statement of faith: (translated, beginning) *There is no deity but God, and Muhammad is the Messenger of God.*

The West Bank

This is not where you exchange dollars for shekels though millions of them both have been lost here. It is a sizeable chunk of land that lies west of the Jordan River whose ownership is like a soccer ball, subject to the latest kick. Here is a map from Wikipedia:[19] The picture on the right is of Beit She'an.

---

[19] http://en.wikipedia.org/wiki/West_Bank

From 1517 through 1917, the area now known as the West Bank was under Ottoman rule as part of the provinces of Syria. At the 1920 San Remo conference, the victorious Allied powers… allocated the area to the British Mandate of Palestine. Following the Second World War, the United Nations passed… a resolution which aimed to establish two states within Mandate Palestine. The Resolution designated the territory described as "the hill country of Samaria and Judea" (including what is now known as the "West Bank") as part of the proposed Arab state, but following the 1948 Arab-Israeli War this area was captured by Transjordan (renamed Jordan in 1949). "West Bank" became the name for the area west of the Jordan River. The interim boundary between Israel and Jordan's West Bank was defined in the 1949 Armistice Agreements. Jordan ruled over the West

Bank from 1948 until 1967[20] when Israel obtained it in the Six-Day War.

In 1987 the Arab residents of the West Bank started a 'Throwing off' – Intifada – and the Prime Minister Rabin's government set up a 'two state authority' in 1994 with the Palestinians. However in 2000 Yasser Arafat rejected this solution and called for a new Intifada[21] and the fighting continues. As of February 2013, 131 (67.9%) of the 193 member states of the United Nations have recognized the State of Palestine as sovereign over both West Bank and the Gaza Strip.[22]

Ah, the history of the West Bank is actually a tad more complicated than that.

In his 2004 essay "How to Cure a Fanatic", one of Israel's most famous authors, Amos Oz, argues that the Israeli-Palestinian conflict is not a war of religion or cultures or traditions, but rather a real estate dispute — one that will be resolved not by greater understanding, but by painful compromise.[23]

We drove by Jericho in the distance to the west; it seemed to be a sizeable town. Alex had commented that Jericho was the oldest city in the world, but said he thought there was at least one other that was making the same claim.

Jerusalem is a sprawling seminal city, both ancient and modern, a city of great significance to three major world religions, a city of peace compartmentalized by high walls and punctuated by machine gun fire. It has been called a city of intense prayer torn asunder by abandonment in loathing. We said goodnight to the gals and then Alex delivered us to our hotel, the Grand Court.

---

[20] Ibid
[21] Fodor's Exploring Israel, p 208.
[22] Wikipedia, Ibid.
[23] Oz, Amos, *How To Cure a Fanatic*, (Princeton, Princeton University Press, 2006), p 61.

One author that I've read quite a bit since returning home is the Israeli Etgar Keret. He is one of the best short story writers on the planet these days – I know that's saying a lot, but he is good. In his story *Suddenly, a Knock On the Door* the protagonist, a writer, is interrupted by a knock on the door and he is ordered to tell a story – at gun point. Twice! He tells the second one 'I would have told you a story – you didn't have to use a gun!' "In this country," the man waving the gun explains, "if you want something, you have to use force."

Monday 19th

Our breakfast offered great rolls.

After Alex picked us up in the morning and we drove over the desert mountains to the east of the city – a route we took several times in the next few days. At the day's first stop we visited the Qumran excavation which is about a mile from the northwest end of the Dead Sea and about fifteen miles from Jerusalem. In 1947 the Dead Sea scrolls were found in twenty-six caves in the hills close to this Bedouin village. In the decades since many more documents have been found. Though most of the material is non Biblical, still, scholars deem all the documents significant from many points of view. They have been age-dated to 225 BCE to 33 common era. As Titus and his Roman troops advanced, the Essenes collected and hid the documents to prevent their destruction, and, as many of their group was killed, they had remained in the caves until our times.[24]

The big question was whether these ancient documents would show that our present day copies of the *Old Testament* had been doctored over the centuries for political religious agendas. No significant tampering has been found.[25]

---

[24] Fodor's, loc cit., p. 221
[25] Price, Bill *History's Greatest Mysteries*, pp. 65-69

In the village there is an ancient building from circa 150 BCE, but what that building was is still not clear, for it contains no bed rooms. When the Romans destroyed the Second Temple they also got this building. The prevailing view is that this was a community building. We visited the museum there and saw a short documentary. The museum also contained art sculptures made from salt.

Alex mentioned *Avaha*, a commercial movie that was about Israeli life. I couldn't find one by that title but did find *Obsession Avaha* released the previous year. There was also a 2004 film called *Avaha Colombianit*. And there is a line of Dead Sea skin care products called Avaha.

We drove south on the west side of the Dead Sea - often seeing it in the distance - to visit Masada. In the reception center Alex got us tickets for the cable car while we looked at various exhibits like the model of the palace (see below.) There was a poster for a performance of Bizet's *Carmen* at Masada and Louis got a photo of it.

King Herod had constructed a working settlement here on top of this mountain anticipating that someday he might need a defensive holdout against the Jews or the Egyptians at this inaccessible spot. He built a filtered water systems, walls, gates, and living quarters – even another palace for himself. He, however, never had to use this fortress as such, for the Roman puppet's reign which had started in 37 BCE ended with his death in 4 BCE.[26] And flippant as history can be, it became the stronghold of the Jews against the Romans.

That 4 BCE date of Herod's death seems to conflict with the Biblical account of Herod's order to kill all male children age two or younger in Bethlehem to mitigate the threat he perceived from the prediction of a new king being born there – thus a paragraph of digression is in order. Nailing down the exact date

---

[26] In Pearlman's *Zealots of Masada* he describes how his Jewish subjects hated him and that Cleopatra had her eyes on Judea for her own, p, 11.

of Christ' birth remains contentious, however, "most scholars generally assume a date of birth between 6 and 4 BC."[27]

In the year 73 CE at Masada Herod's earlier misgivings turned to grim reality. The siege lasted six years; 906 zealots against ten thousand Roman soldiers. Their final strategy since the Romans could outlast them was mass suicide: each man killed his family. Only two women had hid and thus survived. So much of what we know of the Masada massacre comes from the historian Josephus who had actually visited the fortification on the mountain. Masada has come to symbolize the heroism of Jewish resistance.

Alex told us that the first synagogue was at Masada as there were none before the destruction of the Second Temple which had served as the main temple – and the only temple. However, "synagogues in the sense of purpose-built spaces for worship, or rooms originally constructed for some other purpose but reserved for formal, communal prayer, however, existed long before the destruction of the Second Temple. The earliest archaeological evidence for the existence of very early synagogues comes from Egypt, where stone synagogue dedication inscriptions dating from the 3rd century BCE prove that synagogues existed by that date."[28]

What a ride we had to the top on Masada! It sure beat walking the four mile narrow "snake path" to the top, which we could see some folks doing from the cable car. Walking through the ruins, the rooms and their various uses, the baths, the kitchens – all were interesting – and amazing. On the southwest side we could look down on the top of Herod's palace complex, about a hundred feet below, sculptured out of the cliff. In the distance we could also see the etched outlines of the three Roman camps in the barren landscape.

---

[27] http://en.wikipedia.org/wiki/Birth_of_Christ#Date_of_birth
[28] Levine, Lee (24 October 2005th) [2000]. *The Ancient Synagogue: The First Thousand Years* (2nd. ed.). New Haven, Conn.: Yale University Press. ISBN 0-300-10628-9, as reported in a Wikipedia article named *Synagogue*.

A model of Herod's three-tiered palace is on the right; the remnants of it and a general overview of Masada can be viewed on the left.

The Dead Sea is famous as being the lowest land elevation on earth – 1400 feet below sea level. Jordan lies on the east, Israel on the west; it is about forty miles long and nine wide. And of course it is famous for its salinity. At the Dead Sea Louis swam and had me take his picture floating and reading a newspaper. Willodean also swam. A lot of folks were applying mud to their bodies for its alleged rejuvenative effects before swimming. I rolled up my pants and splashed the salty water on my wound making it sting like crazy. The shore was dense with very sharp rocks and I found it hard to walk and wade, but many people were.

As Alex drove us back to our hotels in Jerusalem Louis and I decided to forego the optional walking tour through ancient tunnels under Old Jerusalem: we were pretty tired and Alex had given us absolutely no information about them. At our hotel he announced we had a half hour to get ready if we were going on the tunnel tour. Not a word more about where it was, how we would get there, et cetera.[30] We said nothing and he parted as

---

[29] Picture from Moshe Pearlman's The Zealots of Masada, p. 62
[30] "His plan was ... we would have to get to the Tunnel Tour on our own which was probably impossible to do in the time frame. He also

soon as we tipped him. I don't think any of our group did the tunnels; the tips from Louis and I were not remarkably generous. At the end of the long corridors was our room, 534: it felt good to crash for a few minutes!

The beef at supper that night was terrible, so I ordered a Joseph Stella beer to wash it down. That evening I went down to the lobby and listened to a pianist named Gregory; he was playing such tunes as *What a Wonderful World*, *Autumn Leaves*, *Starlight*, a Mozart dance and his *Rondo in C*, and Rachmaninoff's *Prelude in C*.

Tuesday 20th

Today we joined a larger tour group and our new guide was Avi. He told us that Ein Karem, an area is southwest Jerusalem, is probably where John the Baptist was born and that Bethlehem is in Palestine, in the West Bank. We went to the Hadassah Medical Complex Hospital in Ein Karem which is famous for their innovations in robotic surgery as well as stem cell research to visit the famous Chagall windows in its synagogue. Along the path there were colorful and fanciful sculptures. These sparkling stained glass windows depict the twelve tribes of Israel. (Unfortunately, we were not allowed to take pictures.) Marc Chagall envisaged the synagogue as "a crown offered to the Jewish Queen," and the windows as "jewels of translucent fire." The windows were installed February 1962.[31]

At the Israel Museum was a replica model of old Jerusalem as it was in 69 CE before its destruction, showing the 2nd Temple. The museum contains works by famous European artists such as

---

said we would have to pay for it whether we went or not. The next day we called the Tour Office and were able to plead our case to get the charges cancelled. Apparently the date of the reservation had been changed and we were not informed in advance." - Louis

[31] http://en.wikipedia.org/wiki/Hadassah_Medical_Center

Rembrandt, Marc Chagall and Camille Pissarro as well as such Israeli and Jewish artists as Abel Pann and Reuven Rubin. It features many exhibits of Jewish history and culture.

A separate building here is The Shrine of the Book, a white domed structure that symbolizes a lid like those covering the jars where the Dead Sea scrolls were found; the mostly underground building displays the scrolls in glass cases. Inside, looking straight up to the dome's center was an amazing sight. Below, right: model of the Second Temple.

Close by, on "the museum row" is the Bible Lands Museum, opened in 1992 and built by Elle Borowski, a scholar, collector, and philanthropist who was also a Holocaust survivor. The museum explores the peoples and lands mentioned in the Bible.

Near the museums we could see the Knesset, the Israeli parliament building. Israel has seventeen political parties, Avi stated. All books of the Bible except Nehemiah and Ester were found in Qumran, Avi said.

The Vad Vashem Holocaust Museum is built in the shape of a water system, where so many Jews took refuge during World War II, and running along the very peak is a skylight.

An amazing museum, and because it was, it was very crowded. There were thousands of pictures and exhibits and hundreds of video clips to watch. Trying to go as fast as I could it still took a long time to cycle through, as one room lead to another, zigzagging across the long "water ditch". In one room, models of death camps, in another, cut-a-ways with model clay figures showing how crowded the living conditions were. Many of the rooms had glass floors under which were thousands of actual shoes of holocaust victims.

On the way out I spotted the Museum's book store and of course went in. I found and purchased *Rutka's Notebook A Voice from the Holocaust*, a long lost diary of 14-year-old Rutka Laskier which covers a few months in 1943 as she and her family waited for the Nazi *Aktion* – the forced collection and placement into a ghetto in her hometown of Bidzin, Poland.

At home a few months later I read the book: there were sections so upsetting to read that I would have to go back to them later. Rutka's brother, mother and grandmother (plus many more of her extended family) were gassed in Birkenau, a section of Auschwitz. Only her father survived because of his banking skills. From her *Notebook*:

> The little faith I used to have has been completely shattered. If God existed, He would have certainly not permitted that human beings be thrown alive into furnaces, and the heads of little toddlers be smashed with butts of guns or be shoved into sacks and gassed to death.

> I saw how a soldier tore a baby who was only a few months old, out of its mother's hands and bashed his head against an electric pylon. The baby's brain splashed on the wood. The mother went crazy.

When do people pass from thinking reasonably to fanatical logic that allows them to commit such atrocities – to believe they are doing a good, or right thing?

Outside the back of the museum, Avi's instructions on where to meet were vague and several people asked me if I knew where.

We had lunch in an Orthodox church before we crossed behind the walled area around Bethlehem and Ari had to stay behind. I noticed a woman soldier and her AK-47. The city of Bethlehem is Jerusalem's neighbor to the south. It has been under the control of the Palestinians since 1995. Although stable when we were there, the area around Bethlehem has been subject to tense Israeli-Arab protests and exchange of gun fire. Bethlehem is now only eighteen percent Christian, down from fifty.

We walked to the Church of the Nativity which was originally commissioned in 327 CE by Constantine over the site that is still traditionally considered Christ's birthplace. That church was destroyed by fire during in the sixth century CE. A new basilica was built in 565 by the Byzantine Emperor Justinian. I recall inside this church as darkly lit but filled with thousands of hanging glass jewels and then crowding through a small stone pathway with steps leading down to the cold, dim cave and folks struggling to get a look at the fourteen-point silver star, beneath the altar in the Grotto of the Nativity.

The Basilica of the Nativity is maintained by the Greek Orthodox whereas the adjoining Church of St. Catherine belongs to the Roman Catholics. (Later, both Louis and I would remark that the influence of the Greek Orthodox seems even larger in Israel than that of the Roman Catholics.)

In June 2002 Israel decided to build a security "envelope" or wall 26 feet tall around Jerusalem: when it is completed it will be 202 kilometers long. Not only is the barrier wall controversial, but its route is equally so, cutting off some Palestinian sections from the city, requiring its residents to have to go through checkpoints to enter. Israelis say incidents of terrorism have declined, but opponents argue that the barrier is an illegal attempt to annex Palestinian land under the guise of security and violates international law. The ugly wall (pictured below, left) – a constant in-your-face taunt!

We followed the high wall around to Rachel's Tomb (in the Bible she was Jacob's favorite wife) and entered the domed building. Jews make pilgrimage here regularly and there was a reading room where we noted several Jews reading or praying.

That guarded high wall made our jaunt to Bethlehem strange and claustrophobic.

Louis had been trying to get in contact with Yuval from the tour office through Avi, and he was finally able to track the phone number down and give it to Louis as Louis was wanting to be sure about seeing Alexandria and other points later in our trip.

On our way back to our hotel we saw lots of construction cranes in Jerusalem. And we stopped at a gift shop for an hour in one of those tour company opportunities and didn't get to our hotel until 6:30. My bed felt real good!

<u>Wednesday 21st</u>

We were on the bus at 7:45 am. Avi said this would be a hard walking day. When we got off the bus for the West Wall he said he had never seen the line so long. Security check points and guards with guns were everywhere.

There was an English lady in our group named Pat that was very cheerful and upbeat even though she walked with crutches – and most of the time she was able to keep ahead of me! (That's her walking beside "The Wall" in the picture above.)

The Temple Mount in Old Jerusalem is sacred to both Jews and Muslims; to the Jews because this is the sight of their two temples, both destroyed by invading forces, the second in 70 AD. Prophetically it is to be the site of the Third Temple which is to trigger end times. This is the Jews' most holy spot. The golden Dome of the Rock (constructed late in the seventh century) which sits on the Temple Mount is holy to the Muslims as it covers the sacred rock where Muhammad made a miraculous overnight visit with Abraham, (and some scholars believe he ascended to heaven with the angel Gabriel.) And many Jews believe that the stone it covers is *their* Foundation Stone and is of great significance.[32]

The exposed section of the Western Wall (which I read is 187 feet long and 62 feet tall) is popularly referred to as the Wailing Wall – significant because this is the only surviving remnant of the Second Temple. Jews come from around Israel to visit and pray at the Wailing Wall as do others – every day the area is busy with visitors. More than a million notes of prayer are stuck in the wall's crevices each year.[33] We saw a good number of Hasidic Jews in their long black coats, black hats and beards (MIB), but there was absolutely nothing alien about their being there.

After we ascended to the top of the Temple Mount, the Dome of the Rock was close at hand. What a beautiful building this is – perhaps one of the most beautiful on earth. Though the base is octagonal, the dome and many of its measurements was based on the Church of the Holy Sepulchre and its amazing tile on the exterior was added later, in the mid sixteenth century by the Ottoman ruler, Suleiman the Magnificent – and a magnificent job was done!

---

[32] http://en.wikipedia.org/wiki/Foundation_Stone
[33] http://en.wikipedia.org/wiki/Wailing_Wall

We walked the Via Dolores, a street in two parts, very narrow, crowded lanes, the path Christ took dragging his cross – about two thousand feet. I found it very tiring, the uneven ground, the old cobblestones, I was glad I had my cane and I couldn't tarry too much or I'd lose sight of our group. Once I rested against a door frame under a lintel before continuing my uphill wander. Between the Stations (which in many cases churches had been built) was a cornucopia of colorful kiosks with an army of vendors each loudly proclaiming the best wares with the cheapest prices, and many of the touristing army were captured, only to buy their way out of captivity. The struggling Jesus would smile and be proud of all the lucrative activity his jaunt up this hill with a cross would daily yield – do you think?

Later I was surprised when I was reminded there were only fourteen Stations of the Cross: the number had seemed far greater to my stumbling feet!

How many condemned had struggled this very Via, dragging their torture and death rack, prodded by swords of painful authority?

The culmination of Via Dolores is the summit of Calvary where Christ and others died on a cross. It is also the place, traditionally believed, where he was buried and resurrected – thus of seminal importance to Christians.

The Romans built a pagan temple here but Emperor Constantine –the first Christian emperor – ordered it razed and replaced with a church in 325 Common Era. Since then, over the many centuries, this Church of the Holy Sepulchre has been burnt, rebuilt, renovated and expanded to the ancient-to-new wondrous and sprawling structure it is today. According to the Wikipedia article the church's governance is shared among Orthodox, Catholics, Protestants and others.[34] We got to spend an hour or so here – part of it waiting in line to actually see the Golgotha altar – "the holy of holies", trying to absorb its significance –

---

[34] http://en.wikipedia.org/wiki/Church_of_the_Holy_Sepulchre

hard with the elbowing of literally hundreds of pilgrims and tour groups wanting to see all the various treasures…

There were many religious objects lost on my meager knowledge of their history. The illustration below from Wikipedia shows the church and original hill:

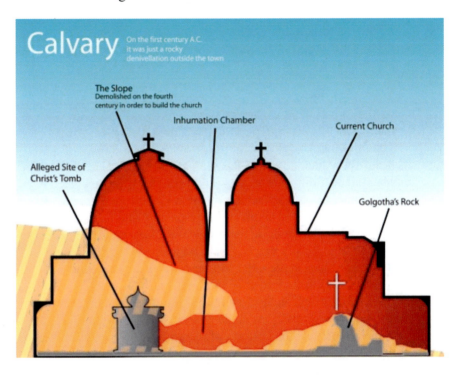

Nearby, on Mount Zion we visited King David's Tomb (though many scholars "don't think it's there" – a phrase I kept running into while researching religious sites around Jerusalem!) and the Cenacle which contains the Room of the Last Supper (ditto on its likely not there.) One thing that is on Mount Zion – though we didn't get to see it – is the Catholic cemetery where Oskar Schindler is buried.[35]

---

[35] http://en.wikipedia.org/wiki/Mount_Zion

The Kidron Valley lies on the eastern side of Jerusalem's Old City separating the Temple Mount from the Mount of Olives. Mary's Tomb is believed to be here (though again others think she died in Ephesus) and various churches have existed on the site since the fifth century.

We stopped at a Kibbutz for lunch. There are three hundred kibbutzim in Israel which have five percent of the population but most of the leaders have come from one. Some are religious, others not, Avi said.

That afternoon as we drove up Mount Scopus which is in the northeast part of Jerusalem (and the highest point is known as the Mount of Olives. The Mount of Olives is due east of the Temple Mount.) As we climbed it we caught glimpses of the beautiful golden domes of the Russian Orthodox Church of Mary Magdalene, built in 1886 by Tsar Alexander III. We visited both the Chapel of Ascension built where it is traditionally believed that Christ ascended earth, and the Roman Catholic Church of the Pater Noster, built on the site where Christ taught his disciples the Lord's Prayer – both on the Mount of Olives. Carmelite Nuns at the latter had made large signs around the walls of the Lord's Prayer in 150 languages. The gardens, the flowers and flittering birds, and the vines surrounding each of those artistic translations made this a favorite stop for me. I could almost feel the holiness of the grounds. Peace was definitely there.

The biblical town of Bethany where the siblings Mary, Martha and Lazarus' home was lies on the southeast slope of the Mount of Olives. Avi was going to take us to the Gethsemane gardens but the road was closed: when he asked the police guard 'Why?', he was told crisply, "None of your business!"

When we arrived back at our hotels we sadly had to say goodbye to our new friends Julie and Willodean. And to Avi who had been a good tour guide. The nice Brazilian couple was staying at our hotel and we said goodbye to them there as well.

Thursday 22nd

We had breakfast and quickly packed, Solomon arriving early to pick us up. We were sharing a van with another, Spanish speaking group – though the new group was small: two groups, two languages, two tour guides.

It was a beautiful clear day. Louis commented again that I wasn't taking enough pictures of him.

We drove north on the road we had used first coming into Jerusalem from Beit She'an and now we passed Jericho again. I had time to think of the places we had visited, so many of them religious sites. Months later as I was working on this journal I came across this amazing story on the internet of a parchment found in a jar at Galilee in a hole long covered with dirt and bushes. The account offers a unique historical perspective and I quote it in entirety here:

From **Simon's Notes**
Recently discovered in a buried urn at a construction site on the Hill of the Beatitudes and now thought to be by a grand nephew of Joseph.

Translated by:
Nedloh Eirual

Whether or not Moses wrote the Genesis story is a matter of conjecture – conjecture, I say, for Moses was a man who could have written it, for it was **not** the *word* of God but the word of a man, and men, we irrefutably know, usually have agendas, and those agendas seldom tally with God.

Like women came from Adam's rib! Good grief: it would be laughable if it weren't so pathetic – and wrong! And these days, immaculate conception – where do they come up with this stuff? Like God would be a big di- and got it on with my Aunt Mary and left my Uncle with all the responsibility and trials of raising his offspring? No, it didn't happen that way.

Uncle Joseph was the father. And a great son he had too. I tire of the disrespect this conception story says about my Aunt – to say nothing of my Uncle –like she'd let any bloke passing by claiming to be God jump in the sack with her, huh? I know, this is just an invented story to put Jesus and his mother above the fray and lay.

Son of God? As if I – and all living people and animals – aren't sons or issue from God. Jesus: flesh and blood by great Uncle Joseph and Aunt Mary, spirit by God. Like everyone I know.

But God talked to Moses, Genesis says. So? He talked to Aunt Mary, he talked to Uncle Joseph, he talked to me, and he talked to the sea. Mankind believes what it wants to believe – or least what's in their best social interest to believe.

I was told from highest authority that he created Eve first, not Adam. He was distracted and then he looked at Eve and saw this appendage hanging between her legs, and then forthwith did he hack it off to create of it Adam, only he made the hack a little too deep leaving a permanent mark; he then took the leftover appendage of excess flesh and blew into it with testosterone and hot air - and thus Adam came to be. He looked at his work and said this is good – and it should prove interesting.

He set them in the Garden of Eden and showed them the fruit and fish, the nuts and wildlife:

> *Behold, the Tree of Life* he said. Beware of slithering salesmen who try to tell you the world is not yours but theirs, but could be yours for a price, he admonished - and of bug-eyed true believers who want to harvest you and your belongings - and was off.
>
> Original sin, of course, was really the snake who created new desire and sold Adam an apple that was already his. Original sin is greed, and nothing at all about sexual matters which is only one of those controlling devices mankind so amply scatters about even more than his seed.
>
> The Second sin, I used to tell my own son Little Jesus, was that snake again saying he did what he did in the name of God. That, and all such proclamations are but the hot air of men.[36]

I wonder whatever happened: it's refreshing that they had such free thinkers back then! At first I thought it was fake, as I don't think they knew about testosterone back then, but then I realized that that was just the translator's phrase for hutzpah.

There was a check point ten kilometers before the border. At the border there was a vehicle security check and we each paid the departure tax of $33.

Louis remarked later that the thing that got impressed upon his mind about Israel was that no matter what church or religious site we visited there just seemed to be boundless American Christians with rapturous looks on their faces as if Jesus was personally watching them with approval…

---

[36] http://www.munchausen_reports/simon

JORDAN

Biblically, the land east of the Jordan River was called Transjordan and in modern times Transjordan was established in 1921 as a British protectorate as a result of World War I and the breakup of the Ottoman Empire. The *Trans* part was dropped in 1948 after Jordan became an independent state.

We had to carry our luggage to a waiting van to shuttle us across the border for five shekel to the Jordan custom house on the Sheikh Hussein Bridge. There we de-shuttled, had to leave our luggage and go inside, and change our money to buy a Jordanian visa which could only be paid for in dinar. The process was quick and efficient and soon we met a new van, our tour guide Archmid and his driver.

Bedouins are the origin of Jordan but still it is a progressive country thanks to the efforts of King Hussein who had ruled from 1952 until 1999 when he was succeeded by his son King Abdulla II. Hussein had been educated in England and was a member of the Royal Air Force. As King of Jordan he worked tirelessly to modernize the country and shore up its economic foundation. After the disastrous Six-Day war with Israel in 1967 he tried to end the age-old Israeli-Arab problems through negotiations with Israeli Prime Minister Yitzhak Rabin, and refused to join Syria and Egypt in the 1973 Yom Kippur war.

In her book, *Nine Parts of Desire*, Pulitzer Prize winning author Geraldine Brooks describes how she once flew into a Bedouin village in a helicopter piloted by King Hussein and went on to relate how this ancient land became the geographical Jordon:

> Winston Churchill used to boast that he created Jordan on a Sunday afternoon with a stroke of a pen. In a meeting in Cairo in 1921, Churchill and T.E. Lawrence (Lawrence of Arabia) doodled the amoeba-shaped state of Transjordan onto a map…to provide a throne for their

ally, Abdullah, who had helped Lawrence fight the Turks in World War 1.[37]

Our first stop was Jerash which is both a modern city and an ancient one with impressive Roman ruins. The ancient city was also called Antioch in the Greek days and was one of the ten cities known as Decapolis.[38] This was a fairly large city in its day complete with amphitheater, forum, and zoo known as Jerashic Park where they actually had a brontosaurus on display that had lasted up to the days of Richard the Lionhearted who was in the area during the Third Crusade, and had it captured and taken to Scotland where it was released into Loch Ness.[39]

Archeologists claim to have found artifacts as old as 3200bce. Hadrian's arch dates from 29 CE and there is a huge oval plaza and a temple for Zeus. These ruins were large and though I walked around a lot, I had to leave the outer limits to Louis and the others while I sat and admired the well-preserved structures.

By early afternoon we were in Amman, a city of seven mountains and a population of two and half million; Jordan's capital has lots and lots of construction cranes. It is one of the oldest continuously inhabited cities in the world. In centuries past it used to be called Philadelphia. Amman is a very clean

---

[37] Brooks, Geraldine, Nine Parts of Desire, New York, Anchor Books, 1996, p. 122.
[38] This was a group of ten cities on the eastern frontier of the Roman Empire in Jordan and Syria. http://en.wikipedia.org/wiki/Decapolis
[39] Not.

city. We drove through Fias Square, the city's center. The country has twenty-two universities, and public schools are free.

Our hotel was modern, named the Grand Palace, which had a security x-ray by the door but we didn't have to use it. They gave us room 504. I noticed the ground floor was "0" in the elevator.

At the hotel supper the drinks were so expensive we didn't buy any.

Someone mentioned the book *Religion for Atheists* by Alain De Botton; I made a note to find a copy to read.

There was controversy on TV news about the black Florida boy shot and the killer not arrested because of the new "Stand your ground" law protecting armed whites against unarmed minorities.

Friday 23rd

The next morning we visited the Amman Citadel which stems from Ptolemy Philadelphia II, ancient ruins high on a hill in the heart of Amman.

Exploring the ruins we came across a large stone hand, its curled fingers waist-high: an earthquake in 749 CE had destroyed this great Hercules statute, now just fragments like the hand are scattered helter-skelter.

We worked our way to the top of the hill where we could see modern Amman below. There was a National History Museum there which had artifacts dating back 6500 BCE. The Citadel mosque dates from 700 CE.

At the entrance of these ruins were three stone tablets outlining the ages, one each for Rabbath-Ammon, Philadelphia, and Amman. There seems to be some overlap of dates which I can't explain:

Rabbath-Ammon	Pottery Neolithic	5500-4500 BC
	Chalcolithic	4500-3300 BC
	Bronze Age	3300-1200 BC
	Iron Age	1200-539 BC
	Persian	539 – 332 BC
	Hellenistic	332 - 63 BC
Philadelphia	Nabataen	312 – 106 BC
	Roman	63 BC – 324 AD
	Byzantine	324 – 635 AD
Amman	Umayyad	661 AD – 750
	Abbasid	750 – 969 AD
	Fatimid	969 – 1171 AD
	Ayyubid	1171 – 1263
	Mamluk Period	1250 – 1516
	Ottoman Period	1516 - 1917

Back in our mini bus and heading out of the city, I noticed many unfinished houses with concrete supports with rebar tentacles sticking out in preparation of a second or third floor and asked: apparently property was so expensive that many homes were routinely constructed for future floors for expanding families.

The King's Highway is the main ancient road connecting north and south Jordan, today most of it is a freeway. On our way south to Petra we passed through the Plain of Madaba and stopped at Mount Nebo: Moses is thought to have lived here and subsequently buried in 1010 bce.

We stopped at a handicraft center in Madaba, known as 'The city of mosaics'. We had been talking to a couple belonging to the other tour group named Mile and Cathy Ford.

The Byzantine Church of St. George in Madaba was built in 535 AD and contains the famous Madaba Mosaic Map.

> The mosaic map of Madaba is the oldest known geographic floor mosaic in **art history**. It is of major use for ... verification of biblical sites. Study of the map played a major role in answering the question of the topographical location of Askalon ... In 1967, excavations in the **Jewish Quarter** of Jerusalem revealed the Nea Church and the *Cardo Maximus* in the very locations suggested by the Madaba Map.[40]

After crossing miles and miles of stark, dry desert we reached the Petra area. Before we wound around the hills on the modern city of Petra to our hotel, we pulled up at a Bedouin settlement that had a small outside restaurant, an old VW bug without front fenders parked rakishly at the edge of a cliff, and a few feet away, a goat's head on a four foot stick. There were beautifully patterned rugs draped on lines or over tubs. In the distance we could see Montreal Castle higher in the mountains in the town of Shoubak, the first crusade castle in Jordan was built in 1116.

Built by the Nabataens, ancient Petra was strategically located where the King's Highway crossed the Silk Road and was built about 400 bce; the Romans conquered it in the second century AD and profited by its trade for a few centuries but when sea trade increased land trade decreased, and Petra steadily declined. The modern city has a population of twenty-five thousand and has sixty-five hotels – a testament to the drawing power of this ageless city carved into the cliffs. The ruins at Petra were rediscovered in 1812.

---

[40] http://en.wikipedia.org/wiki/Map_of_Madaba

We learned that our bus mates were from Columbia and Argentina.

Our hotel in the city of Petra was built on a cliff with the lobby on top and the rooms cascading fourteen floors below: our room was seven floors down. We had a great view from our balcony. There was wonderful art work in this hotel as well; I took pictures of several of the paintings, the first time, I think, that I'd ever been inspired to do so in a hotel. Did a wash to last me two more days. One of the programs Louis had on our room's television was *Arab Idol*.

<u>Saturday 24th</u>

The next morning after breakfast when our tour bus took us as far as it could, to a staging area where we could either walk from there or have a horse pulled cart take us a far as the Treasury. We would be on our own from there but we were told to let the driver know what time to pick us up. The ride down into and amongst the narrow cliffs known as the *Siq* was jittery on our two-wheeled cart, and the young driver seemed particularly in a hurry. Sometimes the descent path was relatively wide, other times barely wider than our driven conveyance producing a definite sense of adventure. At the end of our ten minute ride our path suddenly curved and we beheld the grandness of The Treasury – Petra's most iconic structure. Here was the façade of a temple perhaps a hundred feet high with two floors of columns with a formal entry flanked by statues of Castor and Pollux, and on the level above a statue of Isis[41] – all sculptured into a cliff! Through the doorway were large geometrically *squared* rooms!

Indian Jones & Last Crusade was partially filmed here. Out of the shaking machine and stretching our backs, Arizona Morgan and Maine Holden stood in awe at the cliff before them. Was

---

[41] The age-old Egyptian Goddess: the contemporary terrorist group, Islamic State of Iraq and Syria better be careful not to provoke her too much… And too, I no longer feel free to chant, "Isis! Isis! Ra! Ra! Ra!"

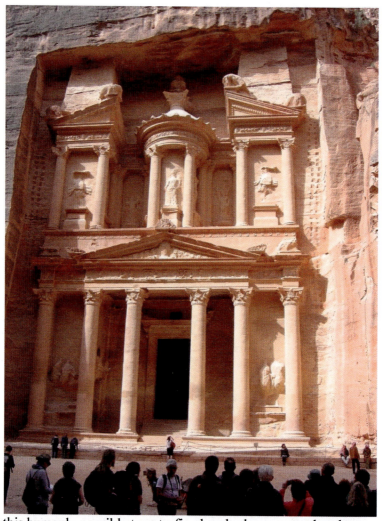

this humanly possible twenty-five hundred years ago that they could do this in a mere decade or two?! Maybe over a thousand years…

As we trudged the three kilometers to the bottom of the canyon and back, most of it was hard going from loose sand causing us to sink in a couple inches with each step – and even the sections of old Roman road that were paved with uneven stones were just as hard. I had to stop frequently for rests. Near the bottom was a three thousand seat amphitheater in fairly good condition. We hiked through areas where general housing had also been carved from the cliffs. Many camels, donkeys and horses passed us, their Bedouin owners ready to give you a ride for a price. I came to appreciate and respect camels at Petra as a number of times I would look up to see a flank of one of these large graceful animals soundlessly passing me only inches away! Not a whisper of a footfall or heavy breathing – just a pleasant look of ageless contentment on their faces, almost a spiritual look of acceptance and service. Only once did I hear a noise from a camel: it was near the bottom of our trek, and the beast was resting on its folded legs: its owner was prodding it with a stick - time to go – and its reply was a negative blat, loud and long enough for emphasis.

At a few places there were makeshift kiosks that offered water and limited refreshments. I saw folks eating yogurt with plastic spoons. There were lots of people, the tourists dressed every which way.

As we made our way down this boulevard between the cliff-city structures, past the various business offices, homes of the rich near the top and those of the middle class midway, then workers' then slaves' modest dwellings at the bottom, my mind was still grappling with how they cut out all those rooms from solid rock. I have trouble imagining how many things are done. Like long playing records: they say there are little bumps in the grooves that when a needle is dragged over them produces a sound. Sound with the subtly and detail of a full symphony orchestra? Sure, tell me another one! Or that you can hide that same sound as microscopic light blips on a compact disk? Nope, not possible! The fact that I have five thousand or so compact discs which I play and enjoy regularly is not sufficient evidence.

It's magic. Just like a television set – which by the way is controlled by a wand!

The wonder of Petra creation? More magic. Or extraterrestrials!

However, since I've returned home and have been working on this journal, another possibility occurred to me: the idea that future mankind invented time travel and came back with future technology and over a few dark nights created this wonder. Why? Certainly for reasons we don't know. Could this and some other amazing structures around the world be part of an experiment? Or an amusement since all normal work in the future is automated, a game like Let's Goose our Ancestors? Can you see the scene of groups of dusty and loosely dressed workers, strange looking droids and drones, and a few uniformed humanoids overseeing construction, one telling a rebellious Petraian not to give him any lipoflavinod? Someday we might know!

Back on track with our trek, there were other fascinating structures that we saw, though none quite equaled The Treasury: the Street of Facades, the Siq, El Deir, Corinthian Tomb; and the Great Temple.

At the bottom discreetly nestled behind some trees was a modest museum with restrooms. Behind this building, and lower, I heard the noise of a loud engine, and investigating saw a tractor with a scoop moving dirt.

Having returned to the Treasury and resting and waiting for our carriage number 8 to arrive and take us to the top there was a cat wandering amongst all the people. I coaxed it over and petted it and the lady on the seat next to me fed it. For a quarter hour or so we gazed upon this wonder of the ancient world and reflected on what it must have been like during the time of its original use.

The painful and bizarre horse and carriage ride from the Treasury up to the entrance was so painfully jarring that it caused me to yelp many times like a cartoon caricature. The young driver giving screeching whistles to make people jump out of his way – even fathers carrying young children on their shoulders – they literally leaping – while our driver whipped the horse mercilessly – it shaking violently with fear as it faltered and strained to gallop without tripping, passing other carriages going the same way amid the horror of screeches and lashes to its side. Was this all to finish quicker to get more business or did he have some private record to break? In any case he was a danger in those narrow paths with a fatality waiting to happen! He obviously didn't care about his horse: I'd never witnessed such cruelty to an animal.

When we got out at the top Louis asked me to contribute to his tip and I refused calling the driver a rectal orifice[42] and he and I got into a short tiff, Louis saying he was just doing his job. The carriages that we dangerously pushed aside to get around – their drivers were doing their jobs: ours was a reckless maniac.

I had wondered about the name, *The Treasury*, and found this explanation on the internet:

> Its Arabic name *Treasury* derives from one legend that bandits or pirates hid their loot in a stone urn high on the second level. Significant damage from bullets can be seen on the urn. Local lore attributes this to Bedouins, who are said to have shot at the urn in hopes of breaking it open and spilling out the "treasure"—but the decorative urn is in fact solid sandstone. Another legend is that it functioned as a treasury of the Egyptian Pharaoh at the time of Moses.[43]

That night back at our Petra hotel I bought computer time so I could send out emails – a half hours' worth for five dollars.

Months later, as I was completing this journal, my daughter and I watched a PBS program entitled, *Time Scanners: Petra* in which a team had probed three areas of Petra with their scanning equipment. The equipment can make computer generated models from billions of measurements accurate to more than a thousandth of an inch. They found evidence of steps at El Deir

---

[42] I think I actually used a vernacular version of this.
[43] http://en.wikipedia.org/wiki/Al_Khazneh

(often called the Monastery) that led them to conclude that it was created from the top down; scans and examination of the South Terrace proved there used to be an Olympic-sized pool there with fountains. (As water was critical to the city, they found numerous channels and cisterns.) Using GPR (Ground Penetrating Radar) they were able to discover tombs in front of The Treasury and a small temple with six columns below and in front of the Monastery. And recently an undisturbed tomb of a Nabataean King was discovered.

Sunday 25th

Louis discovered $150 (three fifties) missing from his money in the hotel's central safe and lodged a complaint with the front desk. They said they would look into it and if they thought the person was guilty, would fire him. Louis asked them to have definite proof before they did that.[44]

Mohammad got us at 8 am and his driver drove fast through the town and along the dangerous hilly curves, but when we got to the main highway on the desert plateaus he slowed down – go figure.

At the Jordan customs we had to drag our suitcases seven hundred feet and pay an exit fee of eight dinar (or twelve dollars.) (Note that we were just a few miles from Egypt as Israel's southern end dips down to a point to Eilat on the Gulf of Aqaba. See map at the front.) At the Israeli entrance customs they were nice while inspecting Louis' luggage. Fifteen miles later we were at the Israeli exit customs where we each had to pay its exit fee again.

---

[44] A similar incident happened to a mutual friend of ours on another trip. By taking only a few bills their crimes often go undetected.

EGYPT

It was 11 am when we dragged our luggage to the Egyptian customs. We ran into a problem here as the custom agent wouldn't sell us a visa, necessary in order to get into the country. Struggling with his English, he told us we would have to get a tourist guide to get us our visa – our Egyptian tour company – Sylvia Tours – was nowhere to be seen – or go back to Eilat, Israel and go to the Egyptian consulate and apply for a visa! (Yes, it'll be ready in ten days…!)

So after the customs officials threw up their hands we sat down to wait and cogitate. And stew; and wait some more. Our hotel for the night was only few hundred feet out the other end of the custom house: so near yet so far… After an hour or so another group came by and we eyed their leader; we saw him talking and carrying on with our custom officers in a way that told us they knew each other very well. Then the new person approached us, his English was good. Saying he was a tour guide from a different company, he essentially repeated the option the custom officer had, which was to go back to Israel; or, we could buy a visa from him for $15 plus a $50 tour company guarantee fee. Going back to Israel would cost us $33 for the exit fee and whatever for taxis… A no-brainer: his offer was the best in town.

So Louis and I dutifully gave him the money in U.S. dollars and we watched as Elee - or whatever his name was, departed with our cash and passports, and even a hopeful smile would not dissipate the gnawing in our stomachs as we wondered if we would ever see them again.

But twenty minutes later Elee was back and our passports had visas in them! We thanked him and exited the building. Our hotel for the night was just to the left and we started for it by the shortest route but a security guard turned to us with his rifle, shaking his head and used his authoritative pointer to indicate the official path.

The Taba Hilton had its own security gate and the two officers seemed friendly and one even called Sylvia Tours for us and subsequently told us they would be here in 2 minutes. (Louis would later remark after a second '2 minute' promise that in Egypt it meant a half hour.) When Sylvia tours arrived they showed us their written instructions which were to pick us up at 3 pm – it was then 1pm.

I waited at the gate and the Sylvia guy asked Louis to show him this mysterious Elee. Later they returned and though Elee hadn't been found the customs people identified him allowing the Sylvia folks to contact him later. So Louis and I piled into the hotel van with our luggage and we started out like we were going somewhere only to come to a sudden stop a hundred feet later. We were at the hotel.

After our luggage was searched by the hotel staff we were issued wrist ID's.

That evening the elevators had stopped working for a while causing Louis who had been swimming in the hotel's very large pool and was in the lobby area at the time, ask where the stairs were. He was shown: they were behind a door marked "PRIVATE"!

The Taba Hotel was right on the Gulf of Aqaba and the view of the Red Sea was fantastic. I took a walk on a picturesque foot path through the gardens along the water. Across the Gulf of Aqaba just a few kilometers looking southeast was Saudi Arabia, and I thought I could see its outline, but without detail. The food was good here as well with a beef dish, turkey, bread, custard banana in caramel sauce, strawberry yogurt... Later I listened to someone calling himself "Mister Hilton" sing various ballads for a half hour before returning to our room. Louis said he noticed a lot of Russian tourists here. Later Mohammed stopped by to tell us we would get our $50 each back in the morning!

Monday 26th

José from Tulsa joined us for breakfast and though we had seen him before in Jerusalem he now became the third member of our small tour group until we departed at the Cairo airport, when we had to catch the plane to Luxor. He was bemoaning the fact that he had paid $220 to visit and climb Mt. Sinai but it looked like the closest he would get was Catherine's Monastery!

Our tour leader gave Louis and I each our fifty dollars back.

Our driver and security guard were both named Abdul and the former was a fast driver. There was also the supervisor, or head of the tour group, Medulla Oblongata.

We whizzed through Taba and its outlying areas before we entered the desert highway with its endless lack of anything but sand – except for an occasional glimpse of the Gulf of Aqaba on our left.

We were told that Moses was at St. Catherine's twice, the first time was marked by the burning bush and God's commandment to him to lead the Israelites out of Egypt, the second, a stay of forty days and nights on Mt. Sinai when God gave him the Ten Commandments.

Saint Catherine of Alexander had been related to Roman royalty and was rich, beautiful and a scholar; she was born in 262 or 282 CE and converted to Christianity in her teens when she reportedly had visions from Christ and Mary; she subsequently visited the Roman Emperor Maxentius to tell him he was wrong to persecute Christians which he didn't take well. After she had converted everyone was sent her way to correct the error of her ways, and he ordered her tortured to renounce her Christianity – possibly on the wheel – thus the origin of the *Catherine Wheel*. Scholars disagree about everything concerning this person – even if she existed at all. Christian tradition has her beheaded around the year 305 and her body transported to Mt. Sinai by angels, others think she escaped from Alexander and disappeared. A couple hundred years later a tomb was found on the mountain and her body was discovered. Or in the year 800 monks discovered her body.

In any case Emperor Justinian I had the monastery built here between 548 and 565 CE on the sight of the burning bush. Saint Catherine's Monastery claims to be the oldest continuous monastery in the world, although an article I read online states that Saint Anthony's to the south of Cairo also makes that claim.

Apparently there had been some trouble for tourists traveling through the Sinai and we were told that our Secretary of State, Hillary Clinton had negotiated an armed escort for American tourists.

Our southerly trek over baked desert was interrupted when we stopped for a break after an hour and a half at a lonely roadside station and store: here an intersecting road would take us (eventually) to St. Catherine's. Rather existentially, beside this handful of dusty buildings was a tall billboard advertising Phoenix Motor Oil. We all went in for a few minutes but Louis forgot his video camera inside: luckily an honest clerk bought it out to us as we were getting ready to leave!

Miles and miles deep into the Sinai Peninsula we stopped at a checkpoint not far from our destination. At St. Catherine's Foley bought us tickets.

We took a taxi for the last mile over a dusty road to the actual monastery. When I say taxi, that's generously speaking, for the forty-odd year old American clunker was missing most of its windows, one of the rear doors, and the rest of the body had clear evidence that brakes on the vehicle had failed various times over decades. It had probably never been parked in the shade for its sunburn made it difficult to determine its original color. Not surprisingly, its driver was rather a wizened character himself.

St. Catherine's Monastery complex is a small, walled oasis set in a narrow desert valley between jagged Mt. Sinai on one side

(2283 meters high) and a high hill on the other. It felt as old as the hills with an intrinsic peacefulness made solid by centuries of tranquil and beneficent prayers and constant goodwill. One could easily believe that God walked its trodden footpaths with pleasure.

Louis took this photo of St. Catherine's with Mt. Sanai looming behind.

The Monastery used to have the oldest known Bible but it was stolen and ended up in the Vatican in the early 1900's. This monastery has the second most important library of church history and literature in the world, the most important being the Vatican of course. There are catacombs under the monastery. Being an Orthodox monastery the complex contains perhaps the world's best collection of early iconic paintings. We went inside Saint Helen's Chapel, dark and mysterious. We were shown the six century door from Emperor Justinian as well as the Fatimid door to an unused mosque. And of course the burning bush, supposedly **The** burning bush witnessed by Moses. It wasn't burning when we saw it though. Here is Louis in front of it. Right: within the walls.

Many people climb Mt. Sinai at night (avoiding the brutal sun) to watch the sunrise from it. My friend Mary Ann was one. There must be an easier side because it sure looked too jagged to climb – especially at night!

In 324 CE St. Peter's Church in Rome was founded and there was the separation of the Egyptian church from Rome. We learned that Coptic means Egyptian. A number of cats called St. Catherine's their home and before we left another kitty presented herself for petting.

The official name of the monastery by the way is the Sacred Monastery of the God-Trodden Mount Sinai.

After our visit, there was a long ride down the Sinai peninsula to Sharm El Sheikh where we stayed the night at the Tropicana Hotel, room 2431.[45] Louis had bought a bottle of rum and he invited Jose over after supper for a drink. Jose had climbed the high hill opposite Mt. Sinai to get a good view of it and pictures.

---

[45] Louis pointed out that this resort city had many gambling casinos, as was the Taba Hilton we had stayed in; gambling is legal in Egypt, unlike most Muslim countries.

He told us that an engine of his Delta jet had stopped during takeoff in New York and the flight had to be aborted.

In 2005 this resort city had suffered a severe terrorist attack: "Eighty-eight people were killed, the majority of them Egyptians, and over 200 were wounded by the blasts, making the attack the deadliest terrorist action in the country's history."[46]

This city (and all of the Sinai peninsula) were under Israeli control after the 6-Day War until it was restored to Egypt in 1982, a period of about fifteen years. There's an Israeli song, *Sharm El Sheikh* by Ron Eliran viewable on YouTube.

Tuesday 27th

Up at 3 am for our early flight to Cairo and Luxor. Louis called for a porter as our unit was a long way from the lobby, and went and knocked on Jose's door. This was the last of my clean clothes! In the lobby we were given boxed breakfasts.

Mohammad who had gotten us our $50's back was there as was Abdul to take us to the airport. At check in they wouldn't allow Louis' extra batteries in his carryon so he had to check the bag. Egypt Air was our airline.

The name Safeya Zaghloul came up – was it on a billboard? In any case, she is known as "the mother of Egyptians." Her dates were 1878-1946; daughter of one prime minister and wife of another, she was a tireless political activist, and after her husband was exiled in 1924 she remained influential in Egypt's Wafd Party of national liberalism for more than another dozen years. Her home was in Cairo.

Cairo airport is huge and modern; we were bussed to our connecting aircraft – about a ten minute ride! Our plane, an

---

[46] http://en.wikipedia.org/wiki/2005_Sharm_el-Sheikh_attacks

Embraer 170 was a Brazilian make. I noted that the two aisles of seats were marked A-C and K-H

This flight was not long: essentially we followed the Nile south. The Luxor airport had a shiny new terminal as well. We got our luggage very quickly. Our tour guide Almad apologized for the local traffic, 'Driving rules are optional here. The only test for a driver's license is whether you can back away from an obstacle!'

Luxor (which name means palms) has about a half million people. Twenty percent of the world's cotton comes from Luxor. The city had its origins as ancient Thebes and came to prominence during the 11th dynasty, and when Montuhotep II unified Egypt it became the capital, remaining the capital during the dynasties of the New Kingdom. Rain in this part of Egypt is extremely rare. One of the guides noted that sometimes more than a year goes by without any at all. Not like soggy Bennu (Phoenix) with its nearly seven inches a year!

The Valley of Kings and the Valley of Queens are located on the west bank near Thebes. The modern city lies on the eastern bank. As do the fantastic temples to Amon-Ra, Karnak and Luxor.

Our boat was the *M.S. Nile Admiral*, painted white and green and was seventy-three meters long. After our luggage was brought aboard by porters, Louis and I settled in.

Later, sitting in a deck chair and taking in the Nile, the longest river in the world, and what I could see of Luxor, it started to sink in that I had finally made it – I was on the NILE with perhaps the oldest documented history of mankind, going back 3000 years before Christ. Though people lived and farmed along the Nile for millennia before that. The historian and scientific journalist James Burke attributes one of the greatest breakthroughs for mankind right here in these parts. He wrote in *Connections*:

The decisive event occurred some time before 4000 bce. when it was noticed…that the river rose and fell regularly once a year… With the early understanding of the annual nature of the flood came an awareness of the need to match human agricultural activity to the cycle, and to harness the retreating waters for use during the dry period. Primitive mud ridges were thrown up to trap the water in basins and ditches were dug from the basins to the fields to carry water on to the growing crops. At about the same time… the digging stick changed its shape; it became a simple scratch plough, with a forward curving wooden blade for cutting the soil, and a backward-curving pair of handles with which the farmer could direct the oxen which replaced men as a source of traction power. This simple implement may arguably be called the most fundamental invention in the history of man, and the innovation that brought civilization into being, because it was the instrument of surplus.

Pharaohs are spread across thirty dynasties divided into **Old Kingdom** (about 2686 – 2181 bce), **Middle Kingdom** and New Kingdom. Only the pharaohs of the New Kingdom are buried in the Valley of the Kings. The **New Kingdom** stretches about five hundred years, from 1570 to 1080 bce. Here is a chronological list of those pharaohs. I've included some facts on a few of them:[47]

Ahmose I		18th Dynasty
Amenhotep I		18th Dynasty
Thutmosis I	ruled from 1528-1510 First pharaoh in the Valley of the Kings	18th Dynasty
Thutmosis II		18th

---

[47] Data for this table is from Dr. Moahmed Nasr, *Valley of the Kings*, pp. 14-17.

		Dynasty
Hatshepsut	This famous Queen ruled from 1490-1483	18th Dynasty
Thutmosis III	ruled from 1490-1436 Expanded Egypt to Syria & Nubia	18th Dynasty
Amenhotep II		18th Dynasty
Thutmosis IV		18th Dynasty
Amenhotep III	ruled from 1405-1367 Built temples in Luxor & Karnak	18th Dynasty
Amenhotep IV	known as Akhenaton, ruled 1367-1350, started single deity Aten, wife was Nefertiti, moved the capital	18th Dynasty
Tutankhamun	ruled from 1347-1339 restored Amun & multi-gods	18th Dynasty
Aye		18th Dynasty
Horemheb		18th Dynasty
Ramses I	ruled 1309-1308, moved capital to the Delta	19th Dynasty
Seti I	ruled 1308-1291, foreign wars	19th Dynasty
Ramses II	ruled 1290-1224, built public works & lots of statues	19th Dynasty
Merenptah		19th Dynasty
Siptah		19th Dynasty
Seti II		19th Dynasty
Amenmes		19th Dynasty
Setnakht		20th Dynasty
Ramses III		20th Dynasty

Ramses IV		20th Dynasty
Ramses V - XI	1161-1090 before the common era	20th Dynasty

As daunting as the various dynasties and pharaohs of Egypt are, its many movements of the capital from city to city had me running to the internet. Here's what Ask.com gave me:

List of Egyptian capitals in chronological order.
- Thinis (Actual Location Unknown) (before 2950 BC) the first capital of Upper & Lower Egypt
- Memphis: (2950 BC - 2180 BC) - I - VIII dynasties
- Herakleopolis: (2180 BC - 2060 BC) - IX and X dynasties
- Thebes: (2135 BC - 1985 BC) - XI dynasty
- Itjtawy: (1985 BC - 1785 BC) - XII dynasty
- Thebes: (1785 BC - 1650 BC) - XIII dynasty
- Xois: (1715 BC - 1650 BC) - XIV dynasty
- Avaris: (1650 BC - 1580 BC) - XV dynasty (Hyksos) XVI dynasty was Hyksos, capital unknown (perhaps in the Kingdom of Kush).
- Thebes: (1650 BC - c. 1353 BC) - XVII dynasty and XVIII dynasty before Akhenaten
- Akhetaten: (c. 1353 BC - c. 1332 BC) - Akhenaten of XVIII dynasty
- Thebes: (c. 1332 BC - 1279 BC) - XVIII dynasty and XIX dynasty before Ramesses II
- Memphis: XIX dynasty during rule of Seti I only
- Pi-Ramesses: (1279 BC - 1078 BC) - XIX dynasty starting from Ramesses II and XX dynasty
- Tanis: (1078 BC - 945 BC) - XXI dynasty
- Bubastis: (945 BC - 715 BC) - XXII dynasty

- Tanis: (818 BC - 715 BC) - XXIII dynasty
- Sais: (725 BC - 715 BC) - XXIV dynasty
- Napata/Memphis (715 BC - 664 BC): The Kushite XXV dynasty rulers were based in Napata, Sudan but ruled Egypt from Memphis
- Sais: (664 BC - 525 BC) - XXVI dynasty
  XXVII dynasty was Persian.
- Sais: (404 BC - 399 BC) - XXVIII dynasty
- Mendes: (399 BC - 380 BC) - XXIX dynasty
- Sebennytos: (380 BC - 333 BC) - XXX dynasty
  XXXI dynasty was Greek.
- Alexandria: (332 BC - 641 AD) Muslim period.
- Al-Fustat: (641 AD - 750 AD)
- Al-Askar: (750 - 868 AD)
- Al-Qatta'i: (868 - 905 AD)
- Al-Fustat: (905 - 969 AD)
- Al-Qahira (Cairo): the present capital (969 AD - Present)[48]

I had no idea!

Above: (l) Salt sculptures, (r) the Wailing Wall

---

[48] http://www.ask.com/wiki/List_of_historical_capitals_of_Egypt

Below is a map that shows some of the ancient place names, e,g., Valley of the Kings and Abu Simbel.

(The above map was found by Louis at
www.globalcitymap.com/egypt/images/egypt-tourist-map.gif)

Thebes:
> ...as the city of the god Amon-Ra, Thebes remained the religious capital of Egypt until the Greek period. The main god of the city was Amon, who was worshipped together with his wife, the Goddess Mut, and their son Khonsu, the God of the moon. With the rise of Thebes as the foremost city of Egypt, the local god Amon rose in importance as well and became linked to the sun god Ra, thus creating the new 'king of gods' Amon-Ra. His great temple at **Karnak** ...was the most important temple of Egypt right until the end of antiquity.[49]

Karnak is a city within a city and the largest ancient religious site in the world. It is a vast complex of temples, chapels, pylons and other buildings. It was started in the Middle Kingdom (2055 to 1650 BCE) and continued through the New Kingdom into the Ptolemaic Period. Approximately thirty pharaohs contributed to its buildings.[50]

Walking through Karnak was awesome – and I don't use that word lightly – it really was jaw dropping meandering among those colossal columns!

There were lots of stray and barking dogs around - and I thought Egypt was supposed to be a cat country!

The great hypostyle hall is 335 by 174 feet; its roof (now missing) was supported by 134 columns 75 feet high[51]: fifty people could stand on the top of each of these columns. Another part of the complex has tremendous obelisks. The largest weighs 328 tons and stands 95 feet tall.[52] How could they have been cut and somehow gotten here from the quarry a hundred miles away? How could they have been erected?

---

[49] http://en.wikipedia.org/wiki/Luxor
[50] http://en.wikipedia.org/wiki/Karnak
[51] The stats on these colossal columns seem to vary by source: these given are from *Egypt* by Abbas Chalaby, 1981, p. 66.
[52] http://en.wikipedia.org/wiki/Karnak

Suppose modern man was given the challenge to remake this temple without the use of wheels, cranes or combustion engines – could we do it?

There's something lacking in our history, and when we figure out how hundred-ton plus blocks of stone could be moved around like movie-set props then our history books may be given a surprising twist.

Ramses II ("the Great") left almost as many statues of himself around Egypt– especially at Abu Simbel – as he had offspring, which our guide said numbered 196; here at Karnak he had the carvings done on the columns. Ramses II reigned in the Nineteenth Dynasty from 1279–1213 BCE and lived into his nineties, longer than any other pharaoh.[53]

Our guide said that between the two temples there were a couple thousand statues.

From Wikipedia: A panoramic view of the great hypostyle hall in the Precinct of Amun Re

The banquet hall with the blue ceiling hails from the 2nd century bce.

---

[53] http://en.wikipedia.org/wiki/Ramses_II

The beetle god Khepry is on the right. A word must be said about ancient Egyptian gods. There are too many to list them all. "In different eras, various gods were said to hold the highest position in divine society, including the solar deity **Ra**, the mysterious god **Amun**, and the mother goddess **Isis**. The highest deity was usually credited with the creation of the world."[54] Ra, the sun, was the source of life and life after death: sunrise = birth and rebirth, sunset = death. Symbolism was big then.

Some of the gods frequently mentioned and depicted in hieroglyphics (besides the three bolded above) are:

> **Anubis** - Jackal-headed god of embalming and watching over the dead
> **Anuket** - The goddess of the Nile River
> **Aten** – The sun disk or globe
> **Horus** – The falcon-headed god most notably being the god of the Sky
> **Khepry** – The scarab beetle, the embodiment of the dawn
> **Ma'at** - The goddess of truth, justice and order
> **Min** - God of fertility, often shown with an erect penis
> **Mut** – *mother*, was originally a title of the primordial waters of the cosmos
> **Naunet** – A goddess, the primal waters from which all arose, similar to Mut

---

[54] http://en.wikipedia.org/wiki/Egyptian_gods

Nephthys – Goddess of death, holder of the rattle, the Sistrum – sister to Isis
Osiris – God of the underworld
Ptah – a creator deity, also God of craft
Sekhmet – Goddess of destruction and war
Seshat - Goddess of writing, astronomy, mathematics & architecture
Sobek – crocodile God of the Nile[55]

We visited the Luxor Temple late in the afternoon so that later we could see this grand temple after sunset when it was dark and dramatically bathed in lights. This temple is south of the Karnak

temple and connected by the Avenue of the Sphinxes which is one and a half miles long. Over the centuries some of the sphinx heads had been replaced by rams heads. In ancient days six stations were set up along this avenue for religious purposes[56] somewhat like those on Calvary hill in Jerusalem.

The photo above is from *Egypt* by Abbas Chalaby. There used to be two obelisks at the entrance, and the missing one

---

[55] http://en.wikipedia.org/wiki/List_of_Egyptian_deities
[56] http://en.wikipedia.org/wiki/Luxor_Temple

can be seen today in the Place de la Concorde in Paris. Here are three more photos taken by Louis inside Luxor Temple:

Handsome guy, isn't he? – Ramses II, I mean.

Pharaoh Akhenaten with his wife Queen Nefertiti tried to change the name of god to Aten from Aman. One step was to move the capital away from Thebes as Aman was the official deity of that city, to Akhenaten (modern Amarna). This move was also a migration away from polytheism to monotheism, while recognizing the existence of many gods but consistently worshiping only one. He said he was the only voice of god (Aten), giving his reign an extra oomph of religious authenticity, but after he died, people just lost touch.[57] His son, King Tut changed the name of god back to Aman – and moved the capital back to Thebes. *Amen* (or Aman.)

History indicates that Nefertiti probably ruled equally with her Pharaoh husband. Nevertheless, her last years are mysterious and there is uncertainty about whether her mummy has been found. According to writer Chris Chibnall, when Dr. Who (who can travel anywhere in space and time) was visiting the Queen in 1334 BCE he gets a distress call from a Space Agency from the year 2367 CE and she decides to accompany him and a big game hunter that he has also picked up from the African plains in the year 1902 (plus the Doctor's regular companions Amy and Rory)

---

[57] Some people saw an apparition at the premier of Philip Glass' opera *Akhnaten* and there was a buzz that it was him: it left early so it probably wasn't.

in a fast pace drama that involves staying ahead of dinosaurs aboard a space arc. The beautiful Queen was both quick and resourceful and saved her companies from sudden death more than once. But it's really obvious that this was sheer fantasy fiction when Nefertiti decides to stay with the chest thumping, macho hunter in his time frame. The real Queen would have never... well, it's obvious![58]

Alexander the Great told the Egyptians that he was a son of Ra: his mother had dreamt it.

Our tour guide pointed out the long gas lines. He told us that the government subsidizes gasoline, and that the price is the same everywhere but distribution differs (military and emergency vehicles exempted.)

Finished the Dirk Pitt book – and a good one it was.

Wednesday 28th

Up at 4:45 am, our room on the boat had quite a tight shower. We visited the west bank and the Valley of the Kings (west symbolized death.) A bus took us across the new bridge where before there used to be only a ferry. The location of the Valley of the Kings was intentionally built away from the river and in

---

[58] Chris Chibnall *Dr. Who: Dinosaurs On a Spaceship*, originally broadcast September 2012.

the foothills of the mountains for both security and flood avoidance.

The old home of Howard Carter was pointed out to us as we drove by: he of course was the relentless English archeologist who discovered King Tut's tomb.

Our tour guide told us that 'No!' in Egyptian was "La-ah" – this to help with the very, very persistent souvenir vendors. He also told us that he wasn't allowed by trade agreements to discourage a "deal," so if he was there and was asked, he would reply "good" for too expensive, and "excellent" for a good buy. No cameras were allowed inside the tombs in the Valley of the King's.

For a period of nearly five hundred years from the 16th to 11th centuries BCE, tombs were constructed here for the Pharaohs and powerful nobles of the New Kingdom. The location of the Valley of the Kings was a secret until the 15th century CE, and then the tombs were subjected to years and years of looting. Sixty-two tombs have been discovered so far, though only twenty were actual pharaohs.

Only the tomb of Ramses IV was totally completed and shows the Gate to the Afterlife; he had started planning and designing his tomb at an early age. It includes a map and instructions – the Book of the Dead – for getting through the twenty-four gates, each having its own guardian. Osiris is the guide after all the gates were passed and in the final judgment one had to have a heart as light as a feather on the balance scale. But where were the locations of afterlife? Why for the ancient Egyptian elite, they were here, in these valleys!

We were shown one tomb as a group and then given a couple hours to explore on our own from those that were currently open. The entrances to the tombs varied in length, art work and preservation, and some of the descending tunnels were hundreds of feet long and (according to the literature) some had ninety degree turns. At the end would be the burial chamber and sarcophagus. Off this chamber on one side would be a well or pit for the collection of drain water.

Slavery was the bitter future of war captives, and they were not allowed in the houses of god (tombs). Stars are the eyes of god and goddesses and the mythology says that the Sky Goddess swallows the sun and sky bringing night, and she, in the form of the beetle Khepry gives birth to the new day.

I visited the tomb of Ramses IX by myself; there was no sarcophagus. Tiring, I took the electric train back to the visitor center. Louis visited the tomb of Ramses VI and was impressed with the art work depicting the boats of the Dead on the ceiling.

One of the ladies from the boat asked one of the young boys hawking his wares why he wasn't in school? The reply: "If you give me money, I'll go to school!" Sincerely.

We visited the Morsey Alabaster Factory where "Four brothers," outside, put on a show that was a mixture of carnival barking and musical – they were good and they were funny – and definitely musical! The lead told (sang in a calypso beat) to one of the more comely lookers in our group – an east Asian - "You have crazy eyes. I want to marry you!" This followed by a chant of "Alabaster, move your body, alabaster…" with backup vocals from the brothers and rhythmic clapping.

Louis was cautioned about taking too many pictures. There was a man behind us sitting on a step of a neighboring building and quietly watching the whole exhibition and smoking through an elaborate – alabaster, do you suppose – bong.

Queen Hatshepsut was regent to Thutmose III but she pulled him off the throne and declared herself the queen and became pharaoh in her own right in 1479 BCE and ruled wisely for twenty-two years. According to Egyptologist James Breasted she is known as "the first great woman in history of whom we are informed."⁵⁹   She concentrated on arts and culture rather than foreign wars, and for that the country prospered. 'My Dad was Aman-Ra and I'm a goddess' she is reported having said.

We visited the wonderful mortuary Temple of Hatshepsut at Deir-el-Bahri on the west side of the Nile (see internet photos above.) It was physically challenging because there were long ramps to climb. Behind the columns were ample engraved works of art. At one time there were three temples here, those of Mentuhotep II of the 11th Dynasty, and Tuthmosis III, Queen Hatshepsut's grandson. They were positioned immediately to the left, but only rubble remains today.⁶⁰ Sadly this area was a scene of a horrible terrorist attack in November 1997, and sixty-two people were killed. The attack so horrified the Egyptian people that sympathy for the fringe Islamic group took a marked plunge.

When resentful Thutmose III finally did take the throne he had all the statues of Hatshepsut taken down or defaced.

Queen Hatshepsut is credited with expanding Egypt's shipping from Nile navigation onward to the seas. From detailed drawings carved in the Temple of Hatshepsut of five ships and other clues, the Nova program, *Building Pharaoh's Ship* follows the re-creation of such a ship and its test on the Red Sea. She became regent of the next pharaoh but she chose to rule in her own right, and one way to gain support would be to get a

---

⁵⁹ http://en.wikipedia.org/wiki/Queen_Hatshepsut
⁶⁰ Siliotti, Alberto, Guide To the Valley of the Kings, pp 97-99

commodity that Egypt used a lot of and that was incense. It was rare and expensive and came from Punt and to get ready supplies of it she needed seafaring ships: thus she built. Historians are still not sure exactly where Punt was, but think it was southeast of Egypt perhaps eight hundred miles. Interestingly, her ships were built along the Nile, disassembled and carried piece by piece across the desert nearly a hundred miles and rebuilt at Mersa Gawasis on the Red Sea.

On the way out one of the vulture boys was chanting, "Post cards! Post cards! Only six million dollars!"

In 1922 Howard Carter and his team opened the tomb of King Tut and when several of his team mysteriously died and there were other bizarre incidents, fears were revived concerning the "curse" of tampering with pharaoh's tombs. Reportedly when Carter sent a messenger to his house after the tomb's first opening, the messenger found Carter's bird cage occupied with a cobra inside with the pet bird in its mouth. Superstitions were fanned and the Curse of King Tut flourished, but Carter himself lived another seventeen years – as did others, helping to quench 'the pharaoh (or mummy's) curse'…

The Anubis, the protector of tombs

We drove by the Colossi of Mammon but didn't get out. Two sitting pharaohs, about sixty-five feet high (but partially decayed) are what are left of a whole avenue of monuments. One of them "sings" every morning at sunrise and wonderful legends were told to explain that, but the truth is that the singing is only a natural phenomenon from the cracked stone.[61] Despite speculation, the song sung is not "God Save the Pharaoh (King)," nor "Cool Waters" but "The Desert Song" which Sigmund Romberg once heard traveling through the area and adapted into one of his musicals. ≠.

We saw more fuel lines and distribution problems. (Louis pointed out later that the fuel lines seemed to be only in southern Egypt, and not in Cairo and Alexandria and wondered if this were a political thing.)

Our last stop was to visit the Isis 2 Papyrus Museum in Luxor, an opportunity to help the Egyptian economy. To be fair, there were beautiful works of art there.

Back on the *Nile Admiral* we were told we would soon be disembarking and that the following night there would be a party and the men were expected to wear a galabiya, the traditional Egyptian robe. Noticed a host of English moms on the boat.

Later, as our large boat slowed approaching the lock at Esna, the vending vultures were lined up on the ramparts on both sides. They threw stuff up to Louis and he bargained with them. They threw up plastic bags with the item to put the money in. They were running along the lock approaches waiting for something to be thrown back or trying to get one's attention, "Excuse me, sie! Excuse me, sei!" over and over. Louis and Mustafa (a particular vendor's name) haggled over a galabiya which he ended up buying for 29 dollars, but he returned at least one thing as time ran out at the lock itself where they weren't allowed. Shore to ship marketing.

On the news: the Pope was visiting Cuba.

That night we heard a thump against the side of our boat – never found out what it was. (Probably a crocodile disdainfully

---

[61] *Egypt*, loc. cit., p. 71

saluting another tourist boat!) We docked and spent the rest of the night on the boat at Edfu.

Thursday 29th

Slept until 7 am, what a luxury! When we got back from breakfast, our beds had been made with the top sheets and blankets and towels folded in an amazing flower arrangement on my bed and a swan on Louis'!

This morning we were supposed to visit the Edfu Temple of Horus but our tour company refused to pay a new, high visitors' fee, so we rested on the decks watching the scenery pass by. (Our tour guide told us that they would substitute something later: Louis thought it was the new Crocodile Museum at Kom Ombo. Maybe.) Every once in a while we could hear the approaching of small motors operating water pumps along the banks.

The news had discussions about the BRICS countries possibly having to bail failed economies in Europe. BRICS is an acronym for an association of five major emerging national economies: Brazil, Russia, India, China and South Africa.

We visited the Kom Ombo ("hill of gold") temple built during the Greek and Roman times which lies about three quarters of the way between Luxor and our cruise destination of Aswan. The patron god of this village was Sobek – the crocodile god – a natural since the bend in the river provided the crocs a favorite place to bask. The temple is actually a double temple joined by a common back wall: the left Twix was dedicated to Horus and the right Twix to Sobek and together they demonstrate (as our tour guide said) how good and evil can live in peace under one roof.

Figures in Egyptian art depicting a key of life known as *ankh* mean the figure is a god ☥. Wings on a sun disk were a symbol for Ra and are frequently found in Egyptian art. Another source said "The god <u>Thoth</u> used his magic to turn Horus into a sun-disk with splendid outstretched wings."[62] Some of the kings depicted here are Roman but dressed as Egyptian.

The ibis was used as a symbol for the god Troth who was the god of justice and fairness. In trials of the day witnesses were commanded to 'Tell the Troth, the whole Troth, and nothing but the Troth' with their hand placed on an icon of an ibis.

Christians had hatred of Romans for the way they were treated (as lion food) so dedicatedly damaged pagan art. Other art was defaced for aniconistic reasons. Thus the art covered by sand over the centuries was saved.

On the back wall of Kom Ombo the art carved showed surgical instruments such as scalpels, suction caps, bone saws, dental tools and medicines. They were advanced in medicine and every temple doubled as a clinic!

Within the complex was a Nilometer, a circular well tool used to measure the Nile's water level.

Making plans for our Saturday trip to Abu Simbel: we would be picked up at 7:30 am and return after 2 pm. Our luggage would be transferred to the sister ship, *Commodore*, and then we would be picked up at 6 pm and taken to the train to go to Cairo.

The *Nile Admiral* arrived in Aswan late afternoon and docked amidst an armada of cruise boats and felucca sail boats. The depth of the Nile here is between six and twenty-four feet and rises six feet in the summer. We could see numerous caves dotting the hillsides not far away.

The latitude of Aswan was an object of great interest to the ancient geographers as it was seated immediately under the

---

[62] http://www.egyptartsite.com/symlst.html

tropic, and that on the summer solstice a vertical staff cast no shadow; and the sun's disc was reflected in a well at noon.[63]

We got our felucca ride, about fifteen of us pouring under the sail onto our boat. Of course several feluccas had to be engaged to accommodate us all. It was fun – *sailing* on the Nile! As had been done by folks for millennia. There was a cool breeze and a bunch of the English moms were on my sail boat. I was able to get a nice photo of one of these boats silhouetted against the setting sun. (See a few pages above.)

That night on the boat there was a Nubian dress supper and dance featuring such dance events as "O' ah Larry", "Yuppi Yuppi", and "Walk the Plank". I had bought a red galabiya for the occasion and enjoyed the dancing. I can't say that I tripped the light fantastic, though I did trip. The party also included variations on 'pass the bottle' and an elimination starting with everyone dancing. Five women were selected for belly dancing and did remarkably well!

Friday 30th

Had a second laundry done via the boat's laundry service to give me enough changes for the rest of the trip.

Our bus took us over the English dam which was built in 1902 and expanded to 150 feet a few years later.

In 1956 the newly elected Egyptian President Nasser seized the Suez Canal; the British, its owner, unhappy about the event, fought back. As he was also planning the construction of a new and much bigger dam and needed foreign help, his timing was perhaps not the best. When the West refused to help he turned to the Soviet Union who gave them a great deal in the early sixties. In 1971 the Aswan High Dam opened four months after he died

---

[63] http://en.wikipedia.org/wiki/Aswan

and the waters started filling in Lake Nasser (also called the Nubian Sea) which would extend for 340 miles.

There were many reasons to build this dam as well as reasons not to, though to most Egyptians the former outweighed the latter. The chief reason for the dam was to control flooding and droughts making agriculture – the major part of their economy – stable. A compelling reason against the dam was all the possible antiquities that would be lost under water, as well as loss of sediments along the lower part of the river vital to agriculture.

It is the second largest earth-filled dam in the world being 364 feet high and over two miles long. The concrete gravity-arch behemoths we have in Arizona, the Hoover and Glen Canyon dams are taller but not bigger in containment, the latter (started in the same year as Aswan) measuring 710 feet high by 1560 feet long.

Nubia is a land older than Egypt itself and sixty thousand families had to be moved from the lake's fill zone.

Our bus parked on top of the dam and we had twenty minutes to explore and view the old English dam in the distance to the north, and beyond that the city of Aswan, and to the south the large reservoir.

The security is tight on the dam for good reason and there were guard stations. A sign on the dam read, "High Dam volume equals 17 times Giza Pyramid." One of the benefits of the new dam is keeping the crocodiles out of the populous lower Egypt. Though we didn't see any, crocs would be clearly seen when they climbed the embankment. After we returned home to the states and I was doing research for this journal, I came across the following story on the internet, and was so amazed by it that it's repeated verbatim here. The article is in English but it's strange that the translator didn't do the Russian name.

By ЛорИ ОЛДЭН

The Nile crocodiles have been a problem for the people of Egypt since way way before the pyramids were built, and that was long time ago, even before Ivan the Great. Anyway, our friends, the Egyptian government, let us know they were looking for ideas to stop them good at the recently built Aswan High Dam. I had worked on the dam project so I knew the area and the problem dem rascally crocs could be, stealing our lunches when our backs were turned – one of the crew had a dog and the crocs got it too. Those creatures are too big and mean to mess with. A lot of them were shot, but they keep coming, way from the bowels of central Africa. I spent hours for days perfecting swift, fully automated way of sending dese crocs back into the Nubian Sea and I'm confidant old Uncle Joe would give his chest a whack in salute for it if he was still alive and our glorious leader.

Here is the plan. You know we have built mighty catapults, eh?: so I, I came up with this Croc'opult. It's the same principle. When they started to climb the slope of the great Aswan Dam, they would be lured by scent of bait like a nice bucket from AFC – Aswan Fried Chicken - into a narrow pathway, and when a croc got to a certain point clamps would grab onto its four legs, the platform with dem on it would rise several feet and swivel to the exact center of the lake; then they would be showed a 46 second film on the proper habits of flight, like no trying to seize birds with their open mouth: a low growl for behavior not good and a snuff through the nostrils for behavior good; then the platform it tilt to a preprogramed angle, and the croc'opult would spring with equal pressure against each of four legs, providing the croc with the thrill of a lifetime, flying three kilometers over the lake to a safe, skipping landing across the water. Even faster than the KGB can send someone to Siberia![64]

The writer went on to say he was turned down without comment.[65]

On the hills approaching the dam from the west is a beautiful sculpture called the Lotus Tower which consists of five gracefully sloping spires connected by a large notched wheel, it was designed by a Russian artist and built in 1971.

One of the problems caused by the dam is a two percent loss of silt through evaporation: a way to get the mud to the agriculture fields below became necessary.

In 1970 a huge effort was made to move the Temple of Philae which started to be submerged to another, higher island about five hundred feet to the north. It is located at the First Cataract of the Nile and thought to be the burial place of Osiris (though there are other contenders.) We visited several of its individual temples. Louis really liked the boat ride to and from, passing the interesting rocky island (see picture above, right.)

This complex is called the Temple of Love and built during the Ptolemy dynasty (2nd century BCE) and is dedicated to Isis.

---

[64] From http:www.russianspring.com.ru The Uncle Joe referred to above is not Sheriff Joe but his mentor, Joe Stalin.

[65] Yet, what of that old poster I saw – at least, I thought I saw – of a crocodile wearing a Captain's hat and vest in the signature colors of Nubian Airlines, gold and olive green, with large sun glasses and a wizened, crooked smile, as it flew over that vast desert sea?

Cleopatra VII (the famous one) was here when she dedicated an addition to the temple she made. Our guide pointed some engraved graffiti in French made in 1799 along one of the back walls.

According to the mythology, the god (or ancient Egyptian king) Osiris who was well loved married Isis who was one of his sisters; his brother Set – the evil one – married his other sister, Nephthys. Set was very jealous of Osiris and murdered him. Then bereaved Isis changed herself and her sister into birds to go search for a suitable coffin, and in their absence, Set chopped the body up into fourteen pieces and scattered them throughout the country so he couldn't be brought back to life. She found all the pieces but one and was able to restore life to him for a single minute. Oh, but what a minute, making love to him and getting herself pregnant with their offspring god, baby Horus!

It was eternal struggle between good and evil. Nietzsche for one listened.

Isis' mother was Nut (not **a** nut.) In art, Isis "is often depicted…nursing the infant Horus. With the advent of Christianity, many of the chapels of Isis were converted to churches, and images of Isis with her baby were reinterpreted to the Virgin Mary holding Jesus."[66]

One of the ever-present venders tried to sell me a blubebe[67] which is a string instrument like an erhu. I would love one, but had no way to get it home.

We were bused to an aroma "essential oils" perfume factory for another opportunity to contribute to the local economy. I don't do well with incense and perfumes. After a few minutes I was finding it hard to breathe so left and sat in the bus. While

---

[66] http://www.shira.net/egypt-goddess.htm
[67] This is only a phonetic spelling. I tried finding a reference for it on the internet – lists of Egyptian musical instruments - to no avail. I even tried calling the Musical Instrument Museum but their specialist for that area of expertize was on leave for several weeks.

waiting I became worried about our bus driver, the only other person on board at the time, as he started talking excitedly on his phone and then stopped and seemed to slump over the steering wheel. I watched carefully and decided I better check on him and was actually half way down the aisle when someone else got on and the driver came to and seemed to act normal.

On the way back to the boat we passed the quarry used for many of the temples and our guide pointed out an unfinished obelisk lying on its side. It had cracked millennia earlier while being cut and had to be abandoned. It would have been the largest ever. It is not known for whom or where it was intended.

We had driven by a beautiful new Coptic church with golden domes a couple of times, but because it was an optional tour for later we didn't get to stop or even slow down to get a picture. The optional tour we had considered but most of it was additional shopping so neither Louis nor I were interested.

That evening on the boat we had a Nubian concert with three instrumentalists, dancers and vocalists.

We said our goodbyes to some of the folks from the boat including two ladies from Hong Kong, and Christie and Danta from Finland. Louis had struck up a friendship with the latter two and spent some time with them.

Spent a little time on the front deck just enjoying the lights and setting, our last night in Aswan.

Saturday 31st

With breakfast behind us and our luggage in the boat lobby we were met on schedule by Handi and his driver Hemo.

The Aswan airport has a modern new terminal with large Egyptian style columns in front. An odd but amusing thing during takeoff: the cockpit door hadn't been securely fastened and it opened and something started rolling down the aisle. Never saw what it was.

As we approached our destination flying over the Nubian Sea, Louis, who had a window seat, said he could see the Abu Simbel below and was able to get a few video feet of it. This was an optional side tour for us and well worth the additional money as it was Louis' all-time favorite place for our trip!

Abu Simbel's monuments were built 3500 years ago by Ramses II and the main attraction are the four colossal statues of him, each about 20 meters tall. For centuries they were important, then people forgot and the sand and winds of millennia nearly covered them until they were rediscovered in 1813 by a Swiss "orientalist" named Burckhardt. UNESCO rescued the monuments from the rising waters from the new Aswan High Dam in an intense effort from 1964 to 1968. The whole mountain with its inner chambers was dismantled into twenty thousand pieces and reassembled higher up the hill. The first block was moved on March 20, 1965 and the water reached the bottom of the old location in September, four months later at the same time as the last block was moved.

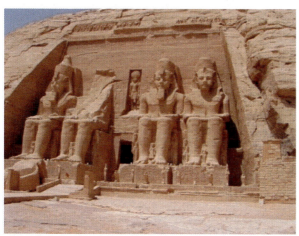

Ramses II ruled for 67 years, had 40 wives of which Nefertari was his favorite. He was embroiled in a long foreign war with the Hittites (in modern Syria) which was going nowhere – the

Battle of Kadesh – so he struck up the world's first recorded peace treaty. When he returned to his throne though, he simply declared (in the form of the god Ra) MISSION ACCOMPLISHED - that he had won, and there was much hoopla and celebration.

Inside the mountain is a large hall lined with eight tall Osiris pillars and various chambers and the furthest one (about 65 meters in) with seated figures of Ra-Horakhty, the deified king Ramses, and the gods Amun Ra and Ptah. On February 22 and October 22 light shines through the door, across the rooms and illuminates three of the four statues. Path, the Prince of Darkness remains in the dark. When they reassembled the rooms the biannual illumination became a day later because of the difference in height. The dates correspond to the king's birthday and coronation day. Others who share Ramses birthday but not his coronation day are: George Washington, Frederic Chopin, Jane Bowles, James Russell Lowell, Edna St. Vincent Millay, Guy Mitchell and Ted Kennedy.

About three hundred feet from the Ramses Temple is the Small Temple dedicated to Nefertari. The statutes here are about half the size; nevertheless this is the only example in Egyptian art where the king and queen are shown with equal size.[68]

Ramses II is the basis for **Percy Shelley's** famous poem "Ozymandias" as well as the inspiration for **Norman Mailer's** *Ancient Evenings* and **Anne Rice**'s *The Mummy*, or *Ramses the Damned*.

Louis had Handi stop at a store when we returned to Aswan so he could buy some Diet Cokes for the train ride. We passed a statue and Louis asked who it was and was told, 'a famous Egyptian writer'. But they didn't know who.[69] When we got aboard the *Commodore* our bags were there as promised. They offered us lunch which I accepted but Louis declined. Later, as

---

[68] http://en.wikipedia.org/wiki/Abu_Simbel_temples
[69] I was able to find two writers who were born in Aswan, Khalil Abdel-Karim and Abbas el-Akkad, so perhaps it was one of them.

we were waiting for 6 pm to roll around we went to the lounge deck. Elvis was singing through the boat's speakers. Louis turned on the TV and I sat down to read. The TV was so loud that I couldn't concentrate so moved to the further end (but it was still bothersome).

I had coffee outside in a covered area by the pool; it was nice in the shade but way too hot in the sun.

Handi was on time and two porters lugged our heavy suitcases up the embankment to where the van was. The train station was not far away and porters again moved our luggage to compartments 17 and 18 in car five. We left mostly on time. The conductor was a nice man and later that night fixed our seats into beds in about thirty seconds!

Sunday, April 1st

I woke at 6:30 am as my nose was both clogged and runny. We had a modest breakfast with lots of rolls. At the Giza Station the conductor came through and said this was where we should get off. John, our new tour guide, his driver Foisy and their boss Samivar were all there to greet us.

John explained that Giza was on the west bank of the Nile, Cairo on the east. We crossed this huge megalopolis (a city of a mere ten million) via an elevated freeway; on the bridge over the Nile we could see Gezira Island home of the Cairo Tower (614 feet high – the highest building in Africa, completed in 1961, and, according to President Nasser, built with U.S. funds)[70] and the Cairo Opera House built in 1988. Our hotel would be on the Avenue of the Pyramids in Giza.

We went directly to Old Cairo.

---

[70] http://en.wikipedia.org/wiki/Cairo_Tower

St Anthony, an early follower of Christ spent much of his life in Egypt. The Romans built a fortress here in the second century. Queen Helen closed the fortress in 313 CE and made the Hanging Church of St. Mary constructed over the two towers. Inside the Hanging Church we were shown a small section of glass floor to show the space between the two towers.

As we were walking through the Old Town, John said many of the houses we were passing were three hundred years old. Old Cairo is also known as Coptic Cairo. We passed through an alley that seemed mostly covered but it charmed me immediately as it was lined on both sides by books for sale: I found books on Cairo and Alexandria and purchased them at the brightly lit souvenir store midway. There was so much neat stuff to look at. I took a photo there of stylized Egyptian cats (see earlier.)

John, a Coptic Christian himself, took us to Abu Serge Church (built in the 15th century) where there was a Coptic mass in process. Over the last few centuries the Egyptian Catholic Church has gained autonomy from the Vatican. They don't have monasteries but do have their own seminary. On January 15, 2013 a new Coptic Pope was elected, Ibrahim Isaac Sidrak. His official title is *Patriarch of Alexandria* though the church is based in Cairo – go figure![71]

We visited the Ben Ezra Synagogue which is built on the site where Moses was found in a basket, and dates to the ninth century and is the oldest synagogue in the city. In the nineteenth century a treasure of abandoned Hebrew secular and sacred manuscripts were found in its store room (called the Geniza documents) and later disbursed to various libraries. We passed by the Church and Nunnery of St. George.

---

[71] "Pope Shenouda III of Alexandria had died on March 17, 2012, right at the time of our trip and there were photos of him everywhere in the display spaces of the Coptic church. His episcopate lasted 40 years, four months, and four days from 14 November 1971." - Louis

The Mosque of Amr was nearby; originally built in 642 CE it is the oldest mosque in Egypt. An Arabic star is two squares, the corners of one intersecting the sides of the other ✦

Though we did not go inside, while writing this report I notice a photo of its interior with hundreds of architraves – an impressive sight though not as impressive as the interior of the Cordoba Mosque-Cathedral we would see the next year.

We visited the wonderful Muhammad Ali Mosque built in 1847, though the old fort – called the Cairo Citadel was built by Saladin - dates back to 1176. This is a huge, beautiful structure. As we climbed the Citadel looking at it on the summit, its large dome and four smaller semicircular domes and towering minarets are very distinctive. Inside and out, the Muhammad Ali Mosque was a highlight of the trip.

Egypt was conquered by the Ottoman Turks in 1517. Economic failures combined with a string of plagues left Egypt vulnerable. Their control waned in part to the continuing power of the Mamluks, the Egyptian military caste who had ruled the country for centuries. As such, Egypt remained semi-autonomous under the Mamluks until it was invaded by the Napoleon I in 1798. After the French were expelled, power was seized in 1805 by Muhammad Ali, an Albanian military commander of the Ottoman army in Egypt.

In 1882 Britain occupied Egypt but the Ottomans held on until November 1914, when it was declared a British protectorate during WW1.[72] Muhammad Ali is considered the builder of modern Egypt, especially scoring a k o with all the schools he built.

Outside this wonderful mosque as we started our descent to where our minibus was parked our view of the city was marred by something Louis and I were quite familiar with – a dust storm! The famous necropolis, Cairo's City of the Dead where today folks actually live and work amongst ancient mausoleum structures was below nearby, and perhaps it was appropriate that our view of it was dusty.

About a kilometer east of the Nile is one of Cairo's most popular spots, Tahrir Square, made famous for the recent revolutionary activities there; and around it sits not only the Egyptian Museum where we were headed but the American University and eleven Ministries.

As I was getting a little shaky and needed to eat, John said he knew just the place, the Museum's café. It turned out to be one of my favorite moments of the trip, sitting there on the perimeter of the square, consuming and an egg sandwich and tea, talking with my friend Louis, and John who was a pleasant and well-informed individual, with near perfect weather at our outside table during this Arab spring day, my eyes taking in the beautiful coral colored museum built in 1901 and to my left the blackened-from-fire skeleton of a medium-rise (about 12 stories) building, the former Ministry of Agriculture, a residual from the recent uprising here, and behind me in Tahrir Square still more folks with signs… it felt like being in a scene of a Graham Greene novel, experiencing the unfolding moments of history.

Not quite satiated with the wonderful ambiance but after my food was consumed, John pushed away from the table as there were miles to go and dreams to see. The Egyptian Museum has the definitive collection of King Tut artifacts.

---

[72] http://en.wikipedia.org/wiki/Egypt

When Howard Carter found the boy king's tomb in 1922 he remarked how the mummy seemed to be burnt; King Tut's death has remained a mystery. A recent article however reveals that scientists examining the body now think that Tut was crushed and killed, possibly in a chariot accident and his body was burned inside his coffin, likely due to a hasty burial and spontaneous combustion of leaked embalming oils.[73]

When we asked why we hadn't seen any women on the staff of the cruise boat it was explained that their families didn't want them away for thirty to forty-five days at a time.

We stopped at Bazaar Kahn Khalili with hundreds of vendors. I had already seen many vendors, plus being somewhat achy and tired, I stayed in the van while Louis and John sampled two or three streets and returned. There was much there to see of course, from the cheapest "Egyptian" souvenirs made in China to the skilled craftsmanship of local artists.

Our hotel on the west side of the Nile in Gaza was the Barceló. We had our suppers in the Nefertari Restaurant. The lentil soup was great.

Somewhere along the way Louis got some great kohlrabi that he raved about.

I had been thinking about visiting my friend Nahla Mattar who was now living in Cairo. I had met her through my daughter Ilana about four years ago. Nahla is a gracious Egyptian composer and while she was earning her doctoral degree in composition at Arizona State University, Ilana had directed the world premiere of her *Scars*, a work for actress and several musicians. In the course of working on *Scars* she had been to our home a few times, and when she wasn't occupied talking with Ilana, I would grab her ear to talk about composers and modern music. After her graduation (which Ilana and I

---

[73] http://www.nbcnews.com/science/crash-then-burn-how-king-tut-died-his-mummy-caught-8C11528450

attended) she returned to Cairo with a teaching job at Helwan University. I was touched and appreciative when she mailed me two compact discs of works by contemporary Egyptian composers! (They are: Abu Bakr Khairat, Yousef Greiss, Hasan Rasheed, Baheega Rasheed, M.Hasan el-Shogaaiy, and Ahmad Ebeid. How great to hear their unique music!)

I had asked John where in Cairo, Helwan University was and he said it was in the southern part. I would have been thrilled to see her – even for just a few minutes, but since I wasn't sure where my hotel would be and what free time there might be I didn't email her beforehand. There in Cairo, I didn't have an actual address or phone number for her, and when we experienced how gridlocked the traffic was it was probably a kind call not to try a meeting – I certainly did not want to disrupt her schedule. Though this would have the best night to try. Sigh…

(After we returned to Phoenix I did email her telling her of my travels and the places I'd seen in Egypt and how I had enjoyed her country so much and wished I could have met up with her. She emailed me back delighted with all the great things I had seen and was pleased that I had thought of her. Dr. Mattar is now curator of the new Umm Kulthum Museum.)

Monday, April 2nd

I was excited because this was our day to drive to Alexandria. Breakfast, however, was sort of marginal.

When we finally got out of the city of Cairo I noticed odd cone-shaped (but rounded off at the top) structures that were about thirty feet high that had many, many circular holes. I asked John what they were and he said they were pigeon cones where farmers raised pigeons, a local delicacy.

John said that Alexander the Great had 34 cities named for him. Alexandria is popular as a summer resort. And that recently it had a large influx of Libyan refugees, a result of their Arab Spring revolution.

I noticed a number of Mobil gas stations, a brand that I used to patronize for years until they left Arizona some years ago. (Left one desert for another, I guess.)

Alexandria is older than Cairo, being founded about 331 years before Christ by Alexander the Great, whereas Cairo was founded in 969 CE by the Fatimid Caliphate, who had created a huge empire (909-1171) that originally started in Tunisia. The death of Alexander the Great from Macedonia marked the beginning of the Hellenistic Age which lasted until 30 BCE with the death of Cleopatra.[74] General Ptolemy, Alexander the Great's closest friend and confidant was made ruler of Egypt even before Alexander's death. The city Alexandria remained the capital under the Ptolemies and through the Roman rule until 640 CE.

As part of my general preparation for this trip I had read *Cleopatra* by Pulitzer Prize winning author Stacy Schiff. Her accomplishments and story make her the most interesting pharaoh of Egypt and not just the Ptolemaic pharaohs. She was, alas, the last pharaoh. Acting on her own she probably could have saved Egypt from the relentless siege of Augustus Octavius Caesar's troops; on her own, I say, and not so emotionally tied to her lover Mark Anthony, a mighty and successful general in his earlier days but after he met the stunning Cleopatra became militarily useless and just wanted to make love not war. He was killed in Alexandria and after his death, Cleopatra grieving, chose to end her life in her own way rather than be paraded through Rome barefoot in chains and rags (as Augustus had done to other conquered leaders.)

Our Cleopatra was actually the seventh to use that name: Seven of Seven – and more amazing than any Borg queen. From

---

[74] Stacy Schiff noted that the Hellenistic Age may "perhaps [be] best defined as a Greek era in which the Greeks played no role." p 9.

childhood she was immersed in studying with the best scholars of the day from the known world. Science, math, drama, literature, governance and languages – she could fluently speak nine, and was the only Ptolemaic pharaoh who could talk directly to the citizens of her country in their own language! She actually had a biology lab – to study poisons and anecdotes. She was the most educated person in her country – and, it seems amazing to think about it - perhaps in her known world! She listened to her people, she talked with them, she held court nearly every day and everyone got a chance to present their grievance or defend their charges.

Alexandria and Egypt prospered under her rule. She was "the greatest deity of the day",[75] respected and loved. As an embodiment of Isis, women had their greatest supremacy with Cleopatra. Unlike her predecessors who spent their time and resources on expanding the empire, Cleopatra wanted quality not quantity, and she became perhaps the greatest pharaoh of them all making her city, Alexander, the most cosmopolitan and cultured city in the known world at the time, surpassing Athens and even Rome which had not hit its highest point yet.

She had her detractors though. Cicero considered himself the greatest wit of Rome and her dominions. When Julius Caesar came to Rome with her for a visit, Cicero got mad. Later he admitted that Cleopatra was better informed and got a lot more laughs at dinners than he did. And a woman too – how unforgiveable! A recent history program decried that she had her brother and sister killed. True, but only after they tried to kill her![76] As a teen a marriage was arranged between her and her younger brother Ptolemy XIII and they were made co-pharaohs. While out on military maneuvers (probably east of the Nile delta) her brother sent a group of troops out to kill her. She got wind of the plan and escaped up the river, and because she could speak the local language, found someone to take her by

---

[75] Schiff, Ibid, p 92.
[76] Schiff relates one other time, after the defeat at Actium when Mark Anthony acted too late, that she had her major detractors killed, fearing the toppling of her throne. P 279.

small boat at night to within a mile or so of her palace and then carry her wrapped in a carpet inside to her personal quarters. Julius Caesar had arrived in her absence and was staying in the palace; she was thus miraculously presented to him from the magic carpet and quickly became his host! He was so smitten that he promptly gave her two children. Ptolemy got wind of his sister's new protector and decided he could win Caesar for himself by lopping the head off Pompey, but the murder impressed Caesar in the wrong way.

In Cleopatra's day (69-30 bce) Alexander boasted over 200 theaters. That's an amazing figure! If I could have my turn in a time ship, I would love to see her Alexandria, the colossal lighthouse, the famous old library stuffed with more scrolls than any other anywhere, and watch Cleopatra holding court, listen to the timbre of her voice, and behold her famous beauty. Yes!

A few miles outside the city, we went through the Alexander Gate.

Our first stop was the Greco-Roman Catacombs (Komei-Shokafa) the largest such catacombs in the country and built on three levels (though the bottom level is now flooded.) Close by was Pompey's Pillar soaring 99 feet into the air, and the ruins of the ancient Temple of Serapis built by Ptolemy III. "The temple became the target of early Christians, and in CE 391 a mob …sacked the Serapeum and its library."[77] Pompey's Pillar was mistakenly so named by medieval travelers: it was actually constructed in the year 300 to honor Roman Emperor Diocletian.[78] There were medium sized sphinxes there as well.

Many of the streets in Alexander were very crowded with the merchant shops spilling into the streets. Many of the taxis were made by Lada, a Russian make.

---

[77] Haag, Michael, Alexandria. Pp. 34-5.
[78] Ibid., p. 35.

Another problem we noticed here as well as in Cairo and asked about was the piles of trash and garbage. Poor John, I know he felt embarrassed about it. He explained that a couple of years ago there didn't used to be a problem and the country had had a program going for years that worked fine until it was contracted out to a company from Spain. They replaced all the existing receptacles with new, but smaller ones and decreased the number of pick-ups: the result was the receptacles immediately overflowed and people just started throwing trash in streets as a protest. The issue was one of the causes of the revolution.

All the Presidential candidates for the upcoming Egyptian elections have promised to go back to the old system.

The National Museum building in Alexandria was the American Consulate until 2000. There were three floors, and what they had was good but they didn't have a lot.

John said the great lighthouse was destroyed in 1326 by an earthquake.

There is a narrow isthmus partially surrounding the East Harbor and Louis and I got to walk along it enjoying the vast blue of the Mediterranean on our left, the harbor on our right with many small boats, and, directly in front of us the Citadel of Qaytbay built by Sultan Qaytbay in 1477. And the many vendors and their often interesting wares. The Citadel is on Pharos Island built at the spot from the fallen stones of the great lighthouse. Here are two shots by Louis:

We had a great lunch (Louis called it the best lunch of the trip!) at Grill Tikka on the second floor with a most fantastic view of the curved beach and city of Alexandria. Such a clear pretty day, and Louis and I had a smorgasbord of eight different humus dips to consume as well as fish (for Louis) and chicken for me while enjoying the bright blue of the Mediterranean and glittering white of the city; the view, the ambiance, the history – all made my mind wander and imagine that instead of Louis opposite me was Justine, that hot beauty of Lawrence Durrell's that symbolized the city's female passion, a character so real she could be here.[79]

Another point of interest were divers practicing their plunges as our restaurant was next door to a diving school!

The astronomer Claudius Ptolemaeus, commonly known as *Ptolemy*, lived and gazed in Alexandria during the second century common era. His *Almagest* was "fairly regarded as the astronomical Bible of the Middle Ages."[80]

We drove along the famous Grand Corniche which follows the circular inner East Harbor passing the Montaza Palace on our way to the new Alexandria library which opened in 2000 (and is next to the University.) So far it has three million volumes, but it hopes to triple that amount. The structure is so ultra-modern that I felt I was just gawking. Inside is as impressive as the outside; wonderful works of art, exhibits of ancient printing presses, banks of computers (2000!), the ceiling with its blue, green and white eye shining light from the outside. It doubles as a research center. "Wow!" escaped from my lips. With its unusual slant-roof design the building is three floors above ground and seven below. Above the library's entrance and flanking most of its side is a large concrete slab with hundreds of mathematical symbols in its façade, that, and an art statue inside are more than just a nod to Alexander's second most famous

---

[79] A quartet of novels set in Alexander of which *Justine* is the first, has become so synonymously associated with this city that they are known as the *Alexandrian Quartet*.

[80] Berry, Walter, A Short History of Astronomy, p. 62

female, Hypatia. Even after the Roman conquest in the year Cleopatra died, 30 bce, Alexander continued to flourish in education and learning and reached its peak with Hypatia, its most famous scholar and teacher. Excelling in mathematics, philosophy and astronomy, scholars came from far, far away to hear her lectures.

The photo on the right by Louis is part of the new library complex, and in the waters just behind it, I understand, are the remains of Cleopatra's palace.

In the year 415, Common Era, a city-wide squabble broke out between Governor Orestes and Cyril, the Bishop of Alexander. There were massacres between Jews and Christians, the governor tried to calm things down and Hypatia made an incidental comment supporting the governor, and that was enough for the excited ignorant element of the Christians who had considered her too knowledgeable and powerful a woman already, so captured and murdered her, cutting and massacring her body with tile shards, a triangular death, bereft of a square foundation or rounded thinking – a triangular death where I'm sure the three points of the holy trinity were conspicuously absent though they may have been murderously exclaimed – "in the name of the Father, the Son and Holy Ghost!".

Some scholars consider this senseless event the end of Classical antiquity and intellectual life in the city.[81] I recently watched a movie titled *Agora* about life in Alexandria leading up to Hypatia's assassination: an exchange between her and the mob seemed to summarize the situation: they refused to question 'the word of God,' and she questioned everything, believing nothing until rigorously proved.

In part of this same complex is an egg shaped theater (planetarium) suspended in a concrete cavity, and a convention center with a large glass front.

Outside, a statue of Demetries Phaleraus (350-280 BCE), the inspiration for the original library, known in its day as the world's best, but tragically burnt to the ground as collateral damage when Julius Caesar ordered the burning of the Egyptian fleet in the harbor. (In Hypatia's day the re-established but smaller library was again burned, this time by mobs.)

---

[81] http://en.wikipedia.org/wiki/Hypatia

The new library is a major point of pride for Alexandrians.

Some of the books in this fascinating library were written by Tawfiq Al-Hakim a native of the city and the writer most credited for putting Egyptian drama on the world map. His *Journal of a Country Prosecutor* is a wonderfully amusing and satiric novel and his play, *Fate of a Cockroach,* is deliciously ironic and witty. Sort of Plato, Orwell, Kafka and Oscar Wilde rolled into one!

We noticed McDonalds and other American fast food restaurants: John said they were open 24/7.

Our ride back to Cairo was interesting but uneventful.

Tuesday 3<u>rd</u>

Our last day of touring! John said June thru September was the flooding season. And canoes of antiquity had been made of papyrus.

We started at 8 and our first stop would be ancient Memphis, founded in 3100 BCE even before the Old Kingdom. Egypt's golden age was the Old Kingdom, when the great pyramids were built.

I asked John if we'd be going by Graceland. Memphis was the first capital of unified Egypt and remained the capital for nine hundred years until the Middle Kingdom when it was moved south to Thebes; it was called the City of White Walls. The king from Upper Egypt welcomed the agriculture and papyrus from Lower Egypt and so agreed to Memphis being their combined capital.

Memphis in its day had a school of art, a military school, and many artful sculptures, and it controlled the traffic on the Nile.

Ptah was their god of arts and engineering at Memphis. His wife also a god, Sekhmet, who was goddess of war and of healing – what a wise combination - and is depicted with a head of a lion; and their son was Nefertum.

The famous Rosetta Stone was inscribed with a decree that established the divine cult of the new ruler Ptolemy V by a congress of priests who gathered at Memphis on March 27, 196 bce. The stone had been moved from Memphis to Rosetta, a town near Alexandria, and was discovered there in 1799. Its top register is in Ancient Egyptian hieroglyphs, the second in the Egyptian demotic script, and the third in Ancient Greek.[82]

Inside the museum there was a statue of Ramses II ten meters tall, lying on its back. It had been excavated in 1820 near the Temple of Ptah. On his shoulders we could clearly see his personal "cartouche". A cartouche is like an oval name plate (in hieroglyphics), usually only worn by pharaohs.[83]

Outside were the ruins of the Great Temple of Ptah, another statue of Ramses II, intact, an alabaster sphinx, and scattered ruins and excavations of the palaces of Apries, Hathor, and Ramses II. Louis spotted an ibis, and we were actually lucky enough to study it fairly closely before it ran out of sight.

Our van took us a short ways to the west to Saqqara, the place for tombs.

While touring the monuments there, a bus load of young women joined the other tourists (including us) each wearing a colorful scarf, or hijab. There are various styles of hijab and different names used throughout Islamic countries such as burka, chador, shayla and others. They vary from full head covering with just slits for seeing to simply covering the hair. In recent years there have been new laws reducing the wearing of hijab, Egypt being

---

[82] http://en.wikipedia.org/wiki/Rosetta_Stone
[83] I wondered if these were the origin of modern name tags worn by military, medical, service other folks.

one. Geraldine Brooks in her book, *Nine Parts of Desire*, said that in Iran the shah's father had banned the chador in 1935 but since the Ayatollah Khomeini years hijab wearing became a way of showing dissidence against the shah's bedfellows, the Americans.[84] Certainly the surge of Islamic fundamentalism in the Arab world has fostered a new – and many would say unhealthy – emphasis on women's coverings.

The Zoser pyramid (the step pyramid) is the oldest building in the world made of limestone, 2860 years BCE; the ziggurat symbolizes the Mountain of Heaven.

The pharaoh's architect Imhotep was a genius in many areas and also the prime minister; he was the first to use limestone and interlocking blocks. He is the earliest known named architect in the world.[85]

The term for a king's rule was five years and only the high priest could grant extensions if the people were happy.

A part of Saqqara is the funerary complex of Djoser (left, below.) It looked so new – was it recently refurbished? It's hard to believe it's as old as the wall and pyramid but could find no information on when it was built.

---

[84] Brooks, Geraldine, *Nine Parts of Desire*, (New York, Anchor Books, 1996), pp 24-25.
[85] Egypt, loc. cit., pp. 39-40.

We stopped at a carpet factory at the edge of a town, and insistent sellers demonstrated their wares. Some of the silk carpets would change color when snapped!

The pyramids at Giza were built on high ground to be seen from Memphis. Among the oldest structures on earth they are amazing. The Great Pyramid is the Pyramid of Khufu and beside it the somewhat smaller Pyramid of Khafre and the modest-sized Pyramid of Menkaure. All together here, there are a number of smaller ones known as Queen's pyramids, and the Great Sphinx.

Of the three, only Khafre's pyramid retains part of its original polished limestone casing, near its top. Louis and I got close to touch some of the large stone blocks of the Great Pyramid and spent a few minutes trying to take it in. Originally 481 feet high with a base width of 756 feet, we stood there looking up, appreciating its massive size! Inside (though we didn't get to see it) are various angled passageways leading to two chambers, the King's and the Queen's.

Back in the '70's I read Erich Von Daniken's controversial book, *Chariots of the Gods?* He, and others, have raised many questions that deserve answers. Here's a couple paragraphs from the book relating to the great pyramid:

> Is it a coincidence that a meridian running the pyramids divides continents and oceans into two exact equal halves? Is it a coincidence that the area of the base divided by twice the height gives the celebrated figure $\Pi = 3.141597$?

> How and with what were the stone blocks cut out of the quarries? With sharp edges and smooth sides? ... 2,600,000 gigantic blocks - how were they transported and joined together to the thousandth of an inch?[86]

There are suggested answers to many of these answers, that are, unfortunately difficult to believe as well, without any pesky extra-terrestrial engineers!

John said the great pyramids were built over 20 years using 18-20 thousand workers, using 2.3 million blocks. Such a number of blocks could make a wall around France three meters high! For millennia the Great Pyramid was the highest structure on earth – until the Eiffel Tower!

A program recently on PBS called *Time Scanners: Egyptian Pyramids* showed how using the latest 3-D scanning technology that literally takes billions of scans, accurate to a thousandth of an inch, that the Great Pyramid is less than one inch off perfect level – even after all these centuries! The program revealed the deep burial chambers below the step-pyramid at Saqqara, and also investigating the Bent Pyramid and the Medium Pyramid, showed how the Egyptians overcame in only a hundred years of these four pyramid's construction, some difficult engineering problems constructing the burial chambers within, due to the massive weight bearing down on them.

After visiting Cleopatra in that time ship I mentioned earlier, I would love to swing back by the construction of the pyramids to see how it actually was done! So much is lost in history. As was the ability to translate the hieroglyphics – until the Rosetta stone was found. And where is Atlantis? – or even Punt?

While I was waiting for Louis and John who went exploring the funerary temple next to the Sphinx, I talked to an old man named

---

[86] Von Daniken, Erich *Chariots of the Gods?* (Bantam Books, New York, 1969), pp 77-78

Abdul sitting by a kiosk. He had been in the Egyptian army three years and met some American military folks.

A PBS Nova program named *Riddles of the Sphinx* had some interesting facts and finds (summarized):

It was typical in ancient Egypt for humans to be depicted with animal heads; there is a huge exception to this: the Sphinx. The Sphinx is built beside the two biggest pyramids so that when the sun sets during the equinoxes it aligns perfectly between them. It is as long as a football field. After a thousand years the Sphinx was nearly buried with sand. Thutmoses IV of the New Kingdom had the Sphinx restored and painted in pop art colors. Controversy over whose face is on the Sphinx has finally been solved: it belongs to Pharaoh Khafre, and not his father, Khufu. After decades of study the most compelling evidence for this conclusion is that the center of the row of twenty-four stones in the Sphinx Temple line up perfectly with the flanks of the Sphinx and the south edge of Khafre's pyramid.

Louis had purchased a Nemes which is the stripped head dress worn by pharaohs. He enjoyed the looks he got while wearing it!

Back at our Giza hotel we said goodbye to John, our favorite guide of the trip. He was a man of great deference – both thoughtful and kind.

Wednesday 4, 2012

Sameil and Fosey picked us up at the hotel at 12:30 am to take us to the airport. We were on an elevated road and passed some very interesting buildings in Cairo along the way. When we had gone about five minutes Sameil had the van go back because they hadn't picked up our boxed breakfasts. The terminal was beautiful but there was double security and we lost our bottled waters, and Louis more of his batteries. (Egyptian security seems tougher on batteries than the U.S.)

There was a half hour delay boarding, apparently because of a large number of wheel chairs.

We had a smooth flight over Greece, Bosnia and Germany to Amsterdam. Then a long, long flight to Portland, Oregon. I listened to a CD of Lang Lang performing Liszt, and Simon Rattle's reading of the Mahler *Second* – both excellent. Also a comedy called Bad Bosses. There was a mother with several children including one about a year old that was teething and fussing. She was so good about keeping the baby's outlook upbeat, playing with him every minute he wasn't asleep. She had started in Kenya. I complimented her on being such a good mother and that she must be exhausted. She looked grateful for the encouragement.

We cruised at forty thousand feet for the five thousand plus miles.

When we got to Portland and went through customs there were no electronic boards telling us which gate our Alaskan Airline flight to Phoenix was at. Odd. The custom officer didn't know, but said they use the "C" area. We had to run because it was boarding time – we found it in a knick of time!

It was a *great* trip seeing the modern cities and cultures built around and from the structures and objectives of the ancient, increasing my personal meager knowledge, and yet, from it all, expanding the awareness of that vast universe of what I do not know.

Still, it was sublime to learn as much as I did!

Dimitri, my proud feline friend, demanded to know if they still worshiped his kind over there in Egypt.

While I was writing this journal I saw a *60 Minute* program that noted Christian communities in the West Bank were under duress and losing people. Israel blames the Muslims. But most of the people interviewed said, no, it was the Israelis.

Recent news had a story of investigators finding a large cut on the throat of Ramses III under the layers of mummy wrap and they now think this was the cause of his death.

Our timing for visiting Egypt was fortunate: the revolution that had ousted Mubarak in February 2011 was quite as Morsi was just getting started and the presidential election was coming a month after our visit, in May 2012. Unrest returned since our trip with his ousting. I was curious about the country's leaders for the last three-quarters of a century or so:

Leader	In power
King Farouk	April 1936 – July 1952 ended revolution
General Nuguib	June 1952 – June 1956 New Republic
President Nasser	June 1956 - September 1970
President Sadat	October 1970 – October 1981 assassinated
President Mubarak	October 1981 – February 2011 forced to resign
President Morsi	June 2012 – July 2013 ousted
Acting Pres. Mansour	July 2013 - June 2014
President el-Sisi	June 2014 – current President

Also, during the writing of this journal I read Professor Amos Oz' collection of three essays, which individually are titled (1) *Between Right and Right*, (2) *How To Cure a Fanatic*, and (3) *The Order of the Teaspoon*. Calling himself a "reformed fanatic," in these short pages he displays astonishing insight, amazing empathy and concise logic. Sometimes the hard answers *can be* absorbed by us human types by just putting things down on paper that are terse facts, with emotions and self-righteousness scrubbed away.

This should be mandatory reading – for all interested in peace and world politics!

As of July, 2014 the news is disheartening with new rounds of shelling and missile exchanges between Israel and Palestine.

BIBLIOGRAPHY

Al-Hakim, Tawfik, *Diary of a Country Prosecutor*, Saqi, London, 2005

Ask.com (individual references noted in text or footnotes)

Bentley, John J IV, *Egypt Guide*, Cold Spring Harbor, NY, Open Road Publishing, 1998

Berry, Arthur, *A Short History of Astronomy*, New York, Dover Publications, 1898

Brooks, Geraldine, *Nine Parts of Desire*, New York, Anchor Books, 1996

Burke, James, *Connections*, N.Y., Simon and Schuster, 1995

Caesarea, Pictorial Guide & Souvenir, Palphot, Herzlia, Israel, n.d.

Casule, Francesca, *Art and History of Jordan*, Florence, Bonechi, 2011

Chalaby, Abbas, *Egypt*, Florence, Bonechi, 1981

Fodor's *Exploring Israel*, New York, Fodor's, 2006

Gilbert, Martin, *Israel, A History*, New York, William Morrow and Company, Inc., 1998

Haag, Michael, *Alexandria Illustrated*, Cairo, American University in Cairo, 2004

Haag, Michael, *Cairo Illustrated*, Cairo, American University in Cairo, 2006

Israel, Pictorial Guide & Souvenir, Palphot, Herzlia, Israel, n.d.

Jerusalem, Past & Present, Palphot, Herzlia, Israel, n.d.

Laskier, Rutka, *Rutka's Notebook, A Voice from the Holocaust*, Yad Vashem & Time, 2008

LIFE, Holy Lands One Place, Three Faiths, New York, Life, 2012

Nasr, Dr. Moahmed, *Valley of the Kings*, n.d., Egypt

Nova, *Riddles of the Sphinx*, PBS, 2013

Nova, *Building Pharaoh's Ship*, PBS, 2013

Oz, Amos, *How To Cure a Fanatic*, Princeton University Press, Princeton, N.J., 2006

Pearlman, Moshe, *The Zealots of Masada*, Palphot, Herzlia, Israel, n.d. (ca 1986)

Price, Bill, *History's Greatest Mysteries and the Secrets Behind Them* New York, Metro Books, 2012

Schiff, Stacy, *Cleopatra, A Life* Back Bay Books – Little, Brown and Company, New York, 2010

Siliotti, Alberto, *Guide To the Valley of the Kings*, Cairo, American University in Cairo Press, 2002

Time Scanners: *Egyptian Pyramids*, PBS, 2014

Time Scanners: *Petra*, PBS, 2014

Vamosh, Miriam Feinberg, *Beit She'an, Capital of the Decapolis*, Israel Antiquities Authority, ERETZ, 1996

Vamosh, Miriam Feinberg, *Megiddo, Armageddon*, Israel Antiquities Authority, ERETZ, 1997

Van Daniken, Erich, *Chariots of the Gods?*, Bantam Books, New York, 1969

Wikipedia (individual references noted in text or footnotes)

PICTURES

(1) Louis at the Beatitudes

(2) Willodean & the Brazilian couple, Silvana and Andre at Mt. Bental café

(3) Louis floating in the Dead Sea

(4) Alex and Julie at the Mt. Bental café

(5) Louis and Julie on the lift to Masada

(6) King Tut-Tut

(7) Maine Holden & Arizona Morgan somewhere in Africa

(8) Tour guide Avi (somewhere in Jerusalem)

(9) Tour guide John (somewhere in Alexandria)

(10) Two Pharaohs in galabiya, one sleepy

(11) Money speaks – even in Jordan - and the lady behind me was amused

(12) Petra conveyance much like the one we used

(13) Alexandria (from Google images) the east end and Grand Corniche

(1) (2) (3)

(4) (5)

(6) (7) (8)

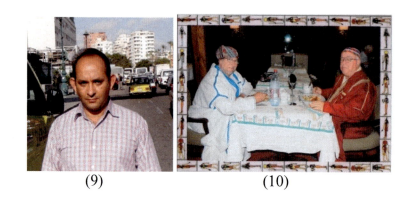

(9)   (10)

(11)   (12)

(13)

A

Abu Simbel · 69
Alexandria · 96
Alexandria library · 99
Alexandria Nationl Museum · 100
Amman · 47
Arab League · 16
Aswan · 82
Aswan High Dam · 83

B

Basilica of Annunciation ·22
Bazaar Kahn Khalili · 95
Beatitudes · 18
Beit Alfa · 26
Beit She'an · 24
Ben Ezra Synagogue · 92
Bethlehem · 36

C

Caesarea · 9
Cairo Citadel · 93
Calvary · 40
Cana · 22
Capernaum · 19
Catacombs Komei-Shokafa · 99
Chapel of Ascension · 42
Church of the Holy Sepulchre · 39
City of the Dead · 94
Cleopatra · 97
Colossi of Mammon · 79

D

Dead Sea · 32
Dome of the Rock · 38

E

Edfu · 81
Egyptian Museum · 94
Ein Karem · 33

F

Felucca · 83

G

Galilee Boat Museum · 22
Golan Heights · 20

H

Hadassah Medical Complex · 33
Hanging Church · 92
Hatshepsut, Queen · 77
Holocaust Museum · 34
Bible Lands Museum · 34

I

Israel Museum · 33

J

Jaffa · 7
Jerash · 47
John the Baptist · 33
Jordan River Park · 21

K

Karnak · 70
Kom Ombo · 81

L

Luxor · 64

M

M.S. Nile Admiral · 64
Madaba · 50
Masada · 30
Megiddo · 12
Memphis · 104
Morsey Alabaster Factory · 77
Mount Nebo · 49
Mount of Olives · 42
Mount Scopus · 42
Mount Zion · 41
Mt. Bental · 20
Mt. Carmel · 8
Muhammad Ali · 94
Muhammad Ali Mosque · 93

N

Nazareth · 22
Nunnery of St. George · 92

P

Petra · 50
Pompey's Pillar · 99
Pyramids · 107

Q

Queen Nefertiti · 74
Qumran Caves ·29

R

Ramses II · 71

S

Saint Catherine · 59
Saqqara · 105
Sea of Galilee · 18
Sharm El Sheikh · 62
Sheikh Hussein Bridge · 46
Shoubak Castle ·50
Sphinx · 109

T

Taba · 58
Tabgha · 19
Tahrir Square 94
Tel Aviv · 5
Temple of Hatshepsut · 78
Temple of Philae · 86
Thebes · 70
Tiberius · 17

V

Valley of the Kings · 64
Via Dolores · 40

W

Wailing Wall · 39
West Bank · 26

Y

Yon Kippur War · 20

About the author

Laurie Holden hails from the deep woods of northern Maine. His first four years were spent at the POW camp at Spencer, the next five in the small towns of Moose River / Jackman and then in the Allagash waterways until high school where he lived in a dorm for four years at Maine Central Institute. He graduated with a BA in English from Northeastern University in Boston in the mid-sixties.

After a year in Hollywood, Florida he decided to move west and picked Phoenix, Arizona. That was in May, 1969 and he has lived there since. His wife Phyllis came with three children, Lorraine, Keith and Amy Gordon. After a few years he and his wife had a daughter, Ilana Lydia, also a writer.

After thirty years with the State as a programmer analyst and writer of policies, standards and procedures he retired. He feels fortunate to have been able to do some traveling abroad as well as writing.